PURBECK

CENTURY

Rodney Legg

DORSET BOOKS

First published in Great Britain in 2002

This book is dedicated to Julia and Matthew Crabb

British Library Cataloguing-in-Publication Data
A CIP record for this title is available from the British Library

The views expressed in this book are wholly those of the author
and not necessarily of the publisher

ISBN 1 871164 495 8

DORSET BOOKS
Official publisher to Dorset County Council

Halsgrove House
Lower Moor Way
Tiverton, Devon EX16 6SS
Tel: 01884 243242
Fax: 01884 243325
email: sales@halsgrove.com
website: www.halsgrove.com

Printed and bound by
Bookcraft Ltd, Midsomer Norton

CONTENTS

INTRODUCTION

Wise words of Thomas Hardy, to the effect that it is better to know one place very well rather than many places just a little, came back to me as I shuffled about in an almost futile attempt to find the precise position where the first Victorian photographer was standing. Where known I'll credit the picture takers, of the main shots ancient and modern, but spare you attribution of smaller ones from after 1970, as they are either mine or by my friend and former partner Colin Graham. Updating the archive has proved an intimate way of studying the landscape. 'Now' pictures also draw the locals out of the woodwork – as the ultimate challenge to Neighbourhood Watch – with the result that all sorts of details have been forthcoming which would never find their way into print in the normal course of events. The process is strangely addictive.

One general observation, made in the wettest month of an awful summer, is that much of our landscape has scrubbed-up to an incredible extent during the past century. What we have lost in the wider landscape to modern agriculture has been at least partially offset by the growth of trees and bushes in and around villages and hamlets. These are often the greenest parts of the countryside. This also applies to the grounds of country houses which were manicured by armies of gardeners until they marched off to war in 1914 and would never look the same again. Our worst example of a totally wiped-out historic view is that of Corfe Castle ruins from Station Road, beside the beer garden of the Bankes Arms, where you can now see zilch. Just fence palings and leaves.

Post Offices are confusing. You soon realise that they have become an endangered species, but even in villages where they survive, such as Bere Regis and Kimmeridge, they have tended to move around. That at Bere Regis comes and goes from three locations in West Street alone and also spent a short time around the corner in North Street.

Wareham Quay still looks nice, to use that inadequate little word, but when it had its mediaeval bridge the setting was wonderful. Its removal in 1926, to ease the way of the motor car, was in the same tragic league as the bureaucratic panic attack that caused the vandalisation of Elizabethan Tyneham House four decades later.

Not all has changed for the worse. While many spots have admittedly lost that photogenic edge others are as wonderful as ever. Tyneham House is now a lost cause but Creech Grange, captured at the very start of landscape photography in 1857, is completely unchanged. Likewise most views of Corfe Castle, or almost so, as my father lost a parked motor-cycle to a chunk of tower masonry which rolled down Castle Hill into Corfe River in the 1920s. Bovington Farm was a surprise as the old map shows it in a different position in relation to the road through Bovington Camp. Then I realised that this had been moved, to round off the corner, and there it was, perfect behind the weeds. Someone's recent bargain from the Ministry of Defence, I was told.

In Worth Matravers I had the uncanny experience of being summoned into a cottage living room to consult the *Dorset Year Book* for 1966–67 – to 'put the record straight' on quarryman Billy Winspit – and found I was being invited to quote from a feature written by one Rodney Legg. 'He was the last to interview and photograph Billy,' I was told. That's typical of the magic and mystery of the Isle of Purbeck which fails to lose its spell and has me going round in ever decreasing circles.

THE PHOTOGRAPHS

PICTURESQUE DORSET.
The Mill & Church, Affpuddle, Dorchester

AFFPUDDLE

Mill and parish church, in a water-colour issued as a postcard – 1904

The view upstream, in an Edwardian painting, looking westwards from the southern of the four 1846-built bridges over the River Frome and its tributaries. Affpiddle or Affpuddle Mill (right) was ignored by the Royal Commission on Historical Monuments, but its history has been painstakingly assembled by local historian Joan Brocklebank. It was owned by Cerne Abbey, appearing in its property schedule of 1356, and surrendered at the Dissolution by Thomas Corton, the last Abbot of Cerne, on 15 March 1539 to Henry VIII's emissary, John Tregonwell. The manor of Affpuddle passed to the Lawrence family, from Creech Grange, and eventually became absorbed into the Frampton Estate.

Their rent books from Moreton House show that John Sare held the Affpuddle Mill and its fishing rights in 1611. Inwood became known as Sares Wood. Future leases were held by John Sanders, Benjamin Drake, William Hooper and William Hall. It was rebuilt in the latter's time, in 1854, and provided with a home-made wheel. This was 'repaired and renewed' in 1877. The mill-house had 'quite gone to pieces' by 1895 and was replaced by the present smaller house. A new steam oven was built for the bakery in 1903. Thatched cottages opposite (left) still gave a rustic look to the setting of St Laurence's parish church, as it was when Thomas Hardy chose it for *The Return of the Native*, where Clym Yeobright marries Eustacia Vye. The tower dates from about 1460.

Musician and historian Joan Brocklebank's memorial seat, in St Laurence's churchyard, was carved by Purbeck sculptor Mary Spencer Watson at Worth Matravers.

AFFPUDDLE

Mill and parish church – 2002 (Rodney Legg)

It far from obvious that this is a photograph of the same spot. Not only have the cottages been demolished and their site incorporated into the churchyard (left) but the disused leet looks more like a ditch, and willows have reduced the view of the church tower to barely a glimpse (centre). Even the bridge has moved a little, having been widened, in 1967.

The Mill House (right) is now a comfortable home. Charles Walter Billey was the miller and baker during the Great War but it Affpuddle Mill seems to have closed after Bladen Bakery opened to the east as part of Ernest Debenham's ambitious enterprises in the 1920s. Joan Brocklebank's study of *Affpuddle in the County of Dorset*, published in 1968, states that the Victorian steam oven and 'some of the wooden geared machinery' were still in the buildings, but this is contradicted by a survey of mills in the *Proceedings of the Dorset Natural History and Archaeological Society* for 1960 (Volume 82): 'All machinery including wheel has gone.' As for water power, the River Piddle hereabouts dried up completely, in the autumn of 1990.

Peony Cottage, dating from early in the seventeenth century, preserves the rural idyll just 100 yards to the south.

Memorial, Briantspuddle

AFFPUDDLE WAR MEMORIAL
Bladen Valley, Briantspuddle – 1955

The War Memorial for Affpuddle parish stands at the entrance to Bladen Valley model village in the nearby hamlet of Briantspuddle. The memorial and south-western cottage are seen from the east in a postcard view. Both were the brainchild of Ernest Ridley Debenham, the London drapery magnate, who started to direct his energies into establishing 'Bladen Farms and Allied Businesses' in 1914, and resumed after the war in 1919. Sir Ernest Debenham, created baronet in 1931 for 'services to agriculture', commissioned sculptor Eric Gill for a modernistic memorial. He worked in Purbeck stone on a stepped plinth and produced a high column which was topped with a square cross. A tall figure of Christ, carrying a sword, faces north. The Madonna and Child, also standing, look south. The text quotes Juliana of Norwich:

South-eastwards from the War Memorial to Old Post House.

> *'To those who fell in the Great War 1914–1919*
> *R.I.P.*
> *It is sooth that sin is the cause of all this pain.*
> *But all shall be well and all shall be well*
> *And all manner of things shall be well.'*

Those of the parish who failed to return were Private Harry Bishop of the Cameron Highlanders; Lance-Corporal Reginald James Budden of the Queen's Own Dorset Yeomanry; Private Bertram Leonard Cox of the Somerset Light Infantry; Private William George Clifford Cox of the Royal Marine Light Infantry; Stoker Frederick Thomas Farr aboard HMS *Invincible*; Private Walter Edwin Goldring of the Machine Gun Corps; and Private Arthur Nicholas Lucas of the 1st Battalion, Dorsetshire Regiment. I am told that the latter perished in the notorious gas attack on Hill 60, in the Zwarteleen salient, on 1 May 1915. The sculptor and calligrapher Eric Gill, who passed through Blandford Camp with the Royal Naval Division at Blandford Camp, is remembered for bizarre personal behaviour and inscribing 'Nation shall speak peace unto nation' on Broadcasting House.

AFFPUDDLE WAR MEMORIAL
Bladen Valley, Briantspuddle – 2002 (Rodney Legg)

The three-storey cottage is still there, behind the walnut and other trees, but this is no longer the photogenic angle. Glancing backwards, and up the valley, it retains its looks. The great agricultural experiment, with the first Alfa-Laval milking machines in Dorset, soon became mainstream. There are still Debenhams at East Farm and in Briantspuddle. Sir Francis Neill, chairman of the Bar Council from 1967 to 1971, married Caroline Debenham, the daughter of Sir Piers Debenham. They live in Blackdown House.

South-westwards from the War Memorial into Bladen Valley.

ARNE

Froxen Copse – 1933

The decoy pond beside Froxen Copse, at the northern end of the Arne peninsula, in a view south-eastwards across the dried-up lake bed with Scouts to prove the point in the hot summer of 1933. Dorset has always attracted Scouts, since Robert Baden-Powell chose Brownsea Island for their first camp in 1908, and scoutmaster George Bowes (right) adopted Arne. He returned in 1934 to marry Phoebe Fenn in St Nicholas's parish church. Both were from Devon and Mrs Fenn was the widow of the vicar of Dawlish. Terence Davis, author of *Arne: A Purbeck Parish in Peace and War*, has also identified Jack Hart (centre).

The white ensign planted at Russel Quay by 'Jurors' from Poole, dressed as Nelson's seamen, who landed in 1926 to protect public rights by marching to Redcliff Atwell.

ARNE

Froxen Copse – 1972 (Rodney Legg)

By the third quarter of the twentieth century, land use at Arne had polarised, between expanding nature reserves on one hand and digging for ball clay on the other. Froxen Copse and its derelict duck decoy, with dead oaks dating from the Second World War when sea water broke through from the Wareham Channel, became a dividing line. Pits operated by English China Clays faced heathland leased, and then bought from Encombe Estate, by the Royal Society for the Protection of Birds. The impetus for this, in 1965, was to preserve gorse bushes holding the core population of the Dartford warbler which had been otherwise wiped out as a British all-year breeding species by the intensely cold winter of 1962-63. Planing permission for mining, for deposits of ball clay which outcrop on the shore of Poole Harbour at nearby Russel Point, was granted to Pike Bros, Fayle and Company in 1957. That year, co-incidentally, the Minister of Housing confirmed the designation order establishing the Dorset Area of Outstanding Natural Beauty. The Purbeck mining company was bought out by English China Clays, in a £1,230,000 deal in 1968, and subsequently traded as ECC (Ball Clays) Limited.

Much controversy and a major public inquiry followed with Environment Secretary Peter Shore confirming the mining company's rights. Dr Michael Gane, for the Nature Conservancy, described it as a 'setback for nature'. British Birds magazine denounced it as 'disastrous' and the British Trust for Ornithology as 'a retrograde step'. Terence Davis, in his study of *Arne*, summed up the situation in 2000: 'Yet, in spite of this widespread criticism, the visitor today might well ask what all the fuss was about. These battles and the subsequent victory for exploitation does not appear to be so disastrous. They will look at the achievements of the RSPB, its nature trails and the peace and solitude here. The extraction of ball clay cannot be seen from the village, and the mining company have been very discrete about the extraction. For most people, nature seems to have quietly taken over.'

The Dartford warbler, now Arne's special species, in a Victorian print

BERE REGIS
Southbrook – 1920s

Horses drinking in the ford across the Bere Stream, looking southwards to Rye Hill, beside the road from Bere Regis to Gallows Hill. Horse-drawn water carriers also waded into the stream to fill their tanks. Architectural historian Fred Pitfield, in *The Book of Bere Regis*, describes the bridge at Southbrook as 'a fine brick bridge having splayed parapets with moulded brick copings and terminal piers, a pair of segmental arches in two concentric courses of headers springing above water level, and triangular plan cutwaters. It was probably built in the eighteenth century, and is said to have been repaired in 1806.'

Watercress beds beside the Bere Stream, below Doddings Farmhouse which was rebuilt in 1904.

The stream flows into the watercress beds at Doddings which were established by William Bedford in 1892. He found the natural springs, coming out of the chalk aquifer as artesian wells, were ideal for cultivation of the iron-rich plant which became a teatime favourite in the Midlands and North. A partnership with Arthur Dwight of Chamberlaynes Farm traded as Bedford and Dwight. By 1920 the Jesty family from Roke Farm was involved in the business which became Bedford and Jesty in 1924. Their 'Sylvasprings' brand was the first in Britain for vegetable produce. William Bedford also pioneered the modern method of marketing watercress in bunches. Previously it had been 'packed loose in returnable flat baskets'. Fred Pitfield recalls that these were known as 'flats' with the old mill building at Doddings being known as the 'flat house' because it was used for their storage.

BERE REGIS
Southbrook – 2001 (Rodney Legg)

The replacement bridge at Southbrook, a slab of reinforced concrete with brick parapets, was built during road widening in 1956. Across the road, Bedford and Jesty have extended the distribution side of their business, from the watercress beds to Southbrook. Here a roadside kiosk caters for local sales. The depot at Southbrook has replaced bunching and packing sheds which used to service each group of beds.

Growing up in Bere Regis during the Battle of Britain, young Fred Pitfield left his mark in wet cement, which can still be seen at Southbrook. Decades later, on retirement as a draughtsman, he returned to Southbrook to making a tracing of his handiwork. It depicts the unmistakable profile of a Spitfire from the front-line fighter base at RAF Warmwell which brought cannon fire, vapour trails and the reassuring sound of Merlin engines to Dorset's beleaguered skies.

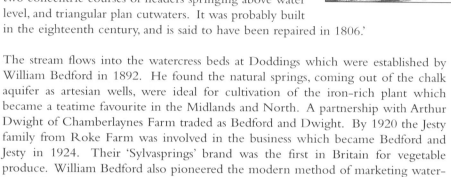

Schoolboy Fred Pitfield's sketch of a wartime Spitfire, in contemporary cement at Southbrook.

WOODBURY HILL, WHERE THE FAIR IS HELD.

BERE REGIS

Townsend Farm – 1908

The northern end of Bere Regis, looking south-eastwards from James Miller's Townsend Farm to Riveridge Wood and Woodbury Hill, 'where the fair is held,' to quote the original postcard caption. Woodbury Hill Fair was one of the great events of the agricultural calendar. Extending over five days, from 18 to 22 September, it took place annually from before 1200 until the Second World War and ceased with a final fair in 1951. Each day had its theme – Wholesale Day (commercial), Gentlefolk's Day (entertainments), Allfolk's Day (entertainments and dealing), Sheepfair Day (livestock) and Pack and Penny Day (dispersal and bargains). When the fair had been and gone, according to local country lore, blackberries were no longer suitable for eating.

Edwardian marquees and stalls at Woodbury Hill Fair, with a glimpse of the chimney of a hilltop building (top right).

Townsend, marking the point at which North Street became a country road to Wimborne, is an eighteenth-century brick and title house. It is said to have been converted into two dwellings by the Wareham Turnpike Trust, in 1765, with the western side being a toll keeper's cottage until the 1870s. The road in the picture was the first turnpike route into Bere Regis, from Wareham via Woodbury Hill, which terminated at Townsend. On the other side of the junction were thatched nineteenth-century barns.

BERE REGIS

Townsend – 2001 (Rodney Legg)

Now the industrial end of Bere Regis, Townsend is separated from the village by playing fields, and the slate-roofed barn (right) is the pavilion for Bere Regis Sports Club. Passing through the middle distance is the eastern arm of Bere Regis by-pass which carries the A35 around the village. It was opened by the Minister of Transport, Mrs Lynda Chalker, on 5 July 1982. The farm moved to the other side of the new road, below Riveridge Wood, with its house and cottages beyond (behind the pole).

Around the corner to the right, set in the hedgerow on the east side of North Street, is a milestone of the Wimborne and Puddletown Turnpike Trust which created the forerunner of the A31 in 1840, together with main road westwards through the Piddle valley. Its figures show the pivotal place Bere Regis had become: 'Dorchester 11, Wimborne 11.' Through much of the twentieth century, at the point where this road met that from Poole and turned from North Street into West Street opposite the Royal Oak, congestion became the norm. One of the first sets of traffic lights in Dorset soon failed to cope with increasing traffic flows.

Barn, now the home of Bere Regis Sports Club, and former Townsend Farm, from the south-west.

BERE REGIS
West Street – 1880

The double bow-windowed frontage of the Post Office, in the time of sub-postmaster Edward Hibbs, looking north-westwards along the north side of West Street to the Drax Arms. On the steps are Mrs Dowland, the post-mistress, and her assistant, Miss Eliza Lane. The Post Office was on the site of the Crown Hotel, which had burnt down in 1788, but for some adverse reason this replacement building was demolished by the end of the nineteenth century. The next shop, No 88 West Street, was occupied by grocer and tailor George Hibbs from 1865 until his death in 1903. It had been the home and business premises of the Case family, who were drapers, tailors and button manufacturers. Fred Pitfield tells us the building had one of the earliest indoor water-closets which was supplied with rainwater from a lead-lined flat roof.

The former King's Arms became the Drax Arms in the 1770s, when James Kitcatt was the tenant. The village's historic Turberville estate had been bought by Henry Drax of Charborough Park in 1733. Samuel and Matilda Strickland succeeded Mrs Cresdee as innkeepers in the 1770s. The first, and so far only, Dorset policeman to be murdered was thirty-eight-year-old Thomas Bishop who was attacked during a drunken riot outside the Drax Arms, at 23.00 hours on 20 September 1877. This was the time of Woodbury Hill Fair. PC Bishop was hit over the head with a large flint. He died at 05.30 the following morning and a twenty-five-year-old labourer, Henry Lock, was charged with murder. His subsequent conviction and imprisonment were for manslaughter. No. 84 was the shop beyond the Drax Arms. Formerly occupied by an ironmonger, James Windsor, it was bought by butcher Thomas Applin.

The Drax Arms and the present Post Office.

BERE REGIS
West Street – 2001 (Rodney Legg)

The vacant space left by the disappearance of the old Post Office has become the front lawn of Cyril Wood House. This provides sheltered housing for elderly artists and was opened by spy-writer John le Carré, the pseudonym of Parkstone-born David John Moore Cornwell, on 16 October 1989. No. 88 is now the Central Stores with both *Echo* placards advertising 'Election Special' editions. The Drax Arms remains in business and the present Post Office is beyond, having replaced the butcher's shop in 1973.

No. 88 West Street (left), as Hatton's Stores on 22 May 1927 (precisely dated from its 'Lindbergh crosses Atlantic' headline) when grocer William Hatton was village sub-postmaster, in a view eastwards to the Royal Oak (centre).

BOVINGTON CAMP

Bovington Farm – 1900 (Walter Pouncy)

The turn of the twentieth century saw the Army arriving in the hamlet of Bovington which had shrunk to a single farmstead on the heath between Wool and Clouds Hill. The view of Bovington Farm is looking westwards along and around what was then the road before it was diverted to the east to round off the corner. The heath was part of the Frampton Estate and the War Office had approached Mrs Louisa Mary Fetherstonhaugh Frampton of Moreton House, in 1896, to buy 1,000 acres for 'a Rifle Range or for any other Military use or purpose'. £4,300 was the eventual purchase price, in February 1899, and Royal Engineers began construction of a 1,000-yard range

Gate-guard provided by a Challenger battle tank at the entrance to the Tank Museum.

with 20 butts. Lieutenant-Colonel George Forty, in *Bovington Tanks*, records that 'some thousand men of the 1st Battalion of the Royal Southern Reserves became the first unit to move into the tented accommodation, when they arrived for their six weeks musketry firing', on 4 June 1900. They were up-staged, however, by the men of B-Company of the 1st Volunteer Battalion, the Dorsetshire Regiment, who came a few hours later. Dorset's home forces became the first to fire shots on the Bovington range. Tanks, which had yet to be invented, would arrive during the Great War.

Meanwhile, agriculture still continued at Bovington Farm and in its meadows to the south, from this eighteenth-century thatched building (left) which has a distinctive plat-band of bricks at first-floor level along its eastern frontage. James Spicer was the farmer for several decades, from before the turn of the century until 1930, who specialised in Dorset Down sheep. His registered flock averaged 250 breeding ewes, 100 ewe hoggets, and five rams. The latter were generally supplied by Henry Jesty of Roke Farm at Bere Regis.

BOVINGTON CAMP

Bovington Farm – 2002 (Rodney Legg)

Despite being on the edge of what became the main-base of the Royal Armoured Corps, the farmhouse at Bovington Farm has survived in a neglected corner of the military complex, with the road having been diverted eastwards. In that direction, on the other side of the replacement road, the buildings of the Tank Museum have mushroomed in recent years. The original idea for a collection of historic fighting vehicles came from author Rudyard Kipling on a visit in 1926 but it was dispersed and partly broken-up during the Second World War. Post-war efforts, by Colonel Forty and his team, gathered 'more tanks than the British Army' and have turned it into one of Dorset's leading tourist attractions.

Royal Tank Regiment memorial at Bovington, prototype model for the bronze unveiled by the Queen in Whitehall Place, 12 June 2000.

Bovington Farm was in a state of limbo when this photograph was taken. It was unoccupied after sale by the Defence Lands Agency for renovation as a house.

BRIANTSPUDDLE

Main Street – 1930

This is a view eastwards from the Crossroads. Briantspuddle hamlet was transformed during the first half of the twentieth century after London department store owner Ernest Debenham, knighted later in life, bought the six surrounding farms from Moreton Estate owner Harry Frampton in 1914. He paid a total of £49,500. Sir Ernest's revitalisation of Briantspuddle was achieved by look-alike architecture that mixed and matched with the existing cob and thatch. New cob was made with a mixture of one third 'tumbled-down cob work, and two thirds chalk'. Numbers 15 and 16 (centre) were his recent addition though the timeless cob-built cottages on either side are from less than a century earlier. Across the road, the wall of Barn Cottage (far left) dated from the eighteenth century. Further along the street, at The Ring, the 100 cow-stall Central Dairy opened in 1919.

The Ring, the centrepiece of Debenham's village, was built in the 1920s as the Central Dairy.

Debenham's village had no public house. The old White Horse in Briantspuddle was a distant memory, and the Four Bells at Affpuddle, which had become four cottages, burnt down in about 1930. The Moor's Head Inn, an off-licence at Briantspuddle, was chosen by Debenham for the site of his new home. Moor Lane House incorporated its road, Moor Lane, as a private drive. An ardent Methodist, Sir Ernest made his hamlet independent of Affpuddle and its parish church. He was tee-total and ordered Vichy water by the crate. The Debenhams continued to be iron-willed. The second baronet, Sir Piers Debenham – a perfect gentleman – broke out from his quiet valley and caused Dorset's most acrimonious hustings of recent times, by standing as an Independent Conservative on an anti-Common Market ticket in 1964. He had the support of the former MP, Viscount Hinchingbrooke, and thereby split the Tory vote. As a result, for the first time, the South Dorset constituency went to the Labour candidate, Guy Barnett. Many of Hinchingbrooke and Debenham's former friends never forgave them.

BRIANTSPUDDLE

Main Street – 2002 (Rodney Legg)

Vegetation again makes it difficult to replicate the precise view. Barn Cottage, the home of the Lieutenant-Colonel George Forty and wife Anne, has been rebuilt in brick (far left). Number 14 (right) carries the name Little Thatch. Numbers 18 and 19 have been extended at the rear. In the other direction, westwards, the Post Office has closed and neither Briantspuddle or Affpuddle now have either a shop or a school. The latter was notable for a young old-boy, Jack Mantle, who moved to Southampton but brought honour to Dorset by continuing firing pom-poms from HMS *Foylebank* in Portland Harbour as she was sunk by Stuka dive-bombers on 4 July 1940. He was posthumously awarded the first Victoria Cross to be won by the Royal Navy in British territorial waters.

The Village Hall and Social Club used to be a barn, built by landowner James Frampton in 1803.

BRIANTSPUDDLE DORSET   28644

BRIANTSPUDDLE
Pheasant Cottage – 1955

The eastern extremity of Briantspuddle, looking along the lane towards Throop, which is the next hamlet. Pheasant Cottage, however, is another of the charming little cottages that is not half as old as it looks. It has been dated to the early nineteenth century. On the other hand, set back from the lane on the northern side towards the Piddle meadows, since expanded outwards and upwards, Cruck Cottage conceals at its heart the genuine cruck-trussed timbers of a low fifteenth-century house.

One of the cottage gardens in Briantspuddle has a mystery stone which was lying in a ditch beside the road junction on Throop Heath, between Affpuddle and Turners Puddle parishes, when it was spotted by Colonel Thomas Edward Lawrence, alias Aircraftman Shaw but better known as Lawrence of Arabia, who was walking with his friend Jock Chambers. Lawrence told him about the tradition of burying suicide victims at night, under crossroads on the no-man's land of a parish boundary, with a stake through the heart. It was known as the Dead Woman's Stone and the alternative local legend was that she had been murdered. Lawrence planned to re-erect the stone in his cottage garden at Clouds Hill. The year was 1934 and his death the following year, after a motor-cycle accident involving a pair of boy cyclists, put an end to the plan. Chambers, however, was determined to achieve Lawrence's wish. He returned to Dorset but found the mystery stone had been moved during the war by Canadian soldiers. On coming back again, at the age of 75 in September 1971, he tracked down the Dead Woman's Stone, apparently to School Lane in Briantspuddle. He offered £100 for it but the offer was refused. A disappointed Mr Chambers returned to his home in Bromley, Kent, 'with the consoling thought that the stone was now preserved and not lying forgotten in a ditch'.

Pheasant Cottage, in a closer view, still with archetypal cob and thatch.

BRIANTSPUDDLE
Pheasant Cottage – 2002 (Rodney Legg)

Dense hedgerows, good for the birds but less attractive to the photographer, again engulf the view. This remains a damper than average environment, which was put to agricultural use in the water-meadows of Affpuddle and Briantspuddle, where the flood-plain of the River Piddle was ditched and sluiced for annual inundation from 1608 onwards. This not only saturated the ground but kept the grass frost-free, enabling quick initial growth in the spring, followed by a dependable second cut of hay for forage and silage. Cruck Cottage also survives and though the cruck timbers are even more hidden away than ever, it does offer the bystander a first-rate floral garden with never a weed in sight. Southwards, along the gravel ridge, trees conceal Culpepper's Dish and a series of smaller geological swallow holes at the edge of the heath, towards the old brickworks and Rimsmoor Pond.

Cruck Cottage lives up to its name, below the thatch, with fifteenth-century roof beams.

CHAPMAN'S POOL

Houns-tout Cliff and Emmetts Hill – 1934 (Ted Legg)

My father took this view of Chapman's Pool, looking south-eastwards from the knoll on the foothills of Houns-tout Cliff. I can date it to 22 June 1934 from the outings listed in his notebook. The boathouses (centre) include a former Lifeboat Station, built in 1867 only yards from the spot where the 400-ton French barque *Georgina* was broken up by the sea in the great gale of January 1866. The station was short-lived, however, and closed in the 1880s. As with that at Kimmeridge the problem was the lack of a suitable settlement near the water for manning the boat with the speed that an emergency demanded.

The crags of Emmett's Hill, towering over the boathouses at Chapman's Pool, in the 1920s.

The big twentieth-century tragedy at Chapman's Pool was the loss of the 5,200-ton freighter *Treveal* on the night of 9 January 1920. Loaded with 8,000 tons of manganese and 2,000 tons of jute, she was on the last leg of her maiden voyage from Calcutta to Dundee. She had put into Portland Harbour for a North Sea pilot but none was available. A navigation error then saw her drifting perilously close inshore, hitting the treacherous Kimmeridge Ledges and splitting in two below Houns-tout Cliff. The 43 crewmen abandoned ship in worsening weather. More might have been saved if they had made a dash directly through the inshore rocks, but they tried to approach Chapman's Pool from further out, where the out-flowing current is stronger than the incoming waves. Their boats were spun broadsides and overturned. Most were battered senseless, despite the heroic efforts of Worth Matravers fisherman Frank Lander and curate Rev. Horace Piercy who pulled several to safety, from the rocks below Houns-tout. Seven were saved; 36 drowned; 15 of the bodies were never recovered.

CHAPMAN'S POOL

Houns-tout Cliff and Emmetts Hill – 1995 (Rodney Legg)

Cattle no longer have access to the cliffs, and the path has been re-routed, so my view is from the 500-feet summit of Houns-tout Cliff. The coastal panorama opens out as you rise to include the plateau that forms the southern tip of the Isle of Purbeck. Known locally as The Plain, this rises to 353 feet, above the choppy race off the rocky shore. St Alban's Head and its Coastguard Cottages and Coastwatch Lookout, with the Norman all-stone chapel dedicated to St Aldhelm standing between them, become the focal point of the view. Shipwrecks remain part of the story. The last major loss of the last millennium, while being towed towards Portland after a collision, was the 6,540-ton freighter *Aeolian Sky* at 04.00 hours on 4 November 1979. En route from London and Rotterdam for Dar-es-Salaam, she went down after the crew had been taken off by lifeboat, 5 miles south-west of St Alban's Head.

Morning-after shot of the Treveal, *split in two but still floating, off Houns-tout Cliff in 1920.*

CHAPMAN'S POOL

Beach and Houns-tout Cliff – 1955

This was Chapman's Pool, firmly a family favourite, as I recalled it. Hairstyles and beach-wear help date the photograph. The other clue is the fact that more people are in the water than on the shore. The summer of 1955 was the best since 1949 and this pattern of wonderful weather was set to continue with an even hotter summer in 1959. Though wild in its setting, and notorious for ledges that were a threat to shipping, Chapman's Pool was regarded as safer than Winspit, and bound to be less crowded than Lulworth Cove. South-facing shallows soaked up the sun and projecting cliffs blocked the winds.

Nina Warner Hooke was a frequent visitor from Langton Matravers. She heard about Sammy the seal, and turned his story into a book, entitled *Seal Summer*. Fisherman Sid Lander, while dropping crab-pots with his son Alan early in May 1961, was the first to see this amazingly friendly grey seal. He came ashore in Chapman's Pool and responded to the hugs and kisses of children, rolling around with them in the sand and shallows, as they kissed and stroked his nose. Whisker-tickling continued until he departed in November.

The former Lifeboat Station and Houns-tout Cliff in another view from 1964.

CHAPMAN'S POOL

Beach and Houns-tout Cliff – 1964 (Rodney Legg)

The inshore view of Chapman's Pool, north-westwards from near the boathouses, has hardly changed since this picture was taken. It stands out in my memory as the last I took in Dorset as a sixteen-year-old, before leaving Bournemouth for Essex to be a reporter in Basildon new town, for my four-year exile. Since then Kimmeridge and Winspit, the next accessible spots around the coast on either side, have become increasingly popular but Chapman's Pool has failed to keep pace. Parking was stopped and you now have to walk. Nature also intervened and active mud-flows made the descent to the beach increasingly messy and difficult. Ted Bowen's description in 2002 sums up the situation: 'The ground has moved and what I remember as a short scramble down a stepped path has become a nightmare triangle of vegetation across a slime of blue mud.'

Distinctive profile of Houns-tout with unstable cliffs beginning to threaten the idyll in 1967.

Hill Bottom gully, created by a stream from below Renscombe Farm, passes through unstable beds of Kimmeridge clay. Bramble and blackthorn smother one landslip as the next opens up beside it. Geology and undergrowth have claimed the original course of the South West Peninsula Coast Path, opened in 1975, which used to drop down to the beach and exit from Chapman's Pool across half a mile of tumbled undercliff below the limestone crags of Emmetts Hill, emerging in deep-cut Pier Bottom beside St Alban's Head. The alternative route goes up and over Emmetts Hill to pass the viewpoint memorial to the Royal Marines.

CHURCH KNOWLE
The Street – 1937

The view eastwards along the village street. Mrs Ivy Wrixon was the shopkeeper at the Post Office (right), telephone Corfe Castle 34, which is seen in a view eastwards along the village street to Knowle Farm House and the Rectory. Rev. Henry Lefroy Russell had been residence since 1926. Knowle Farm House is a substantial two-storey Victorian house with a low-pitched hipped roof.

Opposite is the Reading Room which was provided under the patronage of Rev. Owen Luttrell Mansel to commemorate Queen Victoria's golden jubilee in 1887. The rector's name combined the historic landowning families of Dunster Castle, Somerset, and Smedmore House, Kimmeridge. The Workmen's Club also functioned under the parson's eyes. Ernest White was the secretary in 1937. 'Reading Room' is the inscription above the door but older villagers remember it as the 'Men's Reading Room'. Reading for women was for the home rather than the club.

The latter-day Post Office shortly before closure in 1995.

CHURCH KNOWLE
The Street – 2002 (Rodney Legg)

Numbers 11 and 12, no longer the Post Office, and Knowle Farm House. The Post Office had migrated down the street, towards the New Inn, and finally occupied a stone-roofed extension on the west side of an eighteenth-century thatched cottage. Though modernised this had an interesting ground plan, comprising a living room at the east end, divided by a plank-and-muntin partition from an unheated room. The Royal Commission on Historical Monuments also notes the flat-arched heads of the inner doorway and windows. It closed as a Post Office in 1995 but neighbours Maurice and Rosemary Estop stepped in and provided space in the New Inn. Mrs Pauline Burton-Page, the postmistress from Kingston until 1999, attended for four hours on two afternoons a week.

The New Inn with its name belying the antiquity of a building never known as anything else.

If a hostelry is called the New Inn then one can be reasonably sure that not only will it be a very old building but one that has been licensed premises since beyond living memory. That doubly applies to the stone-roofed New Inn which despite eastern extensions and a recent fire has its origins in a seventeenth-century plan. Once again the Royal Commission has charted the evolution of the building. It began with 'two heated rooms, probably divided by a through passage, and a staircase beside the east chimney-stack'. A blocked doorway and the west window 'each retain a rubble relieving arch'. Re-roofing in the eighteenth century coincided with the building of a northern gable and insertion of a dormer window. Another old building, the thatched former dairy on the east side, has been incorporated, Modern porches and doorways have also been added.

CORFE CASTLE
Afflington Bridge – 1954 (S. F. Aylard)

West Country class 4-6-2 named mainline locomotive 34105 *Swanage*, pushing a train north-westwards, away from its namesake resort. She is heading towards Corfe Castle (top left), which is the next station stop, in a photograph that was used in double campaigns to save both *Swanage* and the Swanage Railway. Built at Brighton in 1950, the engine worked from Bournemouth sheds until the last days of steam on British Railways, being withdrawn to Eastleigh on 12 October 1964. She was hauled from there to Barry Dock scrapyard, in February 1965 by a famous engine, Battle of Britain class 21C151 *Winston Churchill*.

Closer view of the Corfe Castle setting to prove we have one of the most scenic lines in the land.

The line was also down on its luck, pruned by the infamous axe wielded by Dr Richard Beeching, and eventually closed, despite prolonged appeals for a reprieve, in 1972. The track was then lifted with what many of us regarded as indecent haste, which would have made closure irrevocable but for determination of Andrew Goltz, who led the fight to revive the Swanage Railway. He was also instrumental in saving *Swanage* from the breakers though on being rescued she headed eastwards to the Hampshire watercress line between Alton and New Alresford. From an incredible state of dereliction which Colin Graham and I photographed in 1976, the Swanage Railway was put gradually back together, starting at the seaside. It reached the residual track at Furzebrook, rejoining the Weymouth-Waterloo mainline at Worgret. Goltz, the visionary founder of the project, returned on 3 January 2002 to join Wareham ganger Tony Trood in fitting a golden track-screw to link the private company's metals with those of Railtrack.

CORFE CASTLE
Afflington Bridge – 2002 (Rodney Legg)

Scrubbing-up prevents any meaningful attempt at recreating the view along the left-hand bank but on the right the flora still holds sway. Coming from Corfe Castle, this is 4-6-0 class S15 engine 826, which was built at Eastleigh in 1927. She is approaching Afflington Bridge.

This carries a relatively fast section of the A351, between Peaked Close House and Woodyhyde Farm, and has seen several fatal road crashes. In the most recent a car fell on the track and as a consequence the parapets were being extended and strengthened as we went to press in the autumn of 2002.

Ganger sees British Railways class 4MT engine 80104 through the cutting after a road accident at the bridge.

CORFE CASTLE

Bankes Arms Hotel – 1903

The Bankes Arms Hotel, refitted in 1889, is seen from the churchyard, looking north-eastwards to East Hill, opposite the junction of East Street with Station Road (right). Landlord Henry Stickland was followed by Frederick Bulbrook. Their hostelry was named for the family who had owned Corfe Castle and its estate from 1635, when it was purchased by wealthy forty-eight-year-old Attorney General, and later Lord Chief Justice, Sir John Bankes. The previous owner, Lady Hatton, was the widow of Sir Edward Coke. In east Dorset, on the other side of the River Stour, Sir John and Lady Mary Bankes bought the former manorial lands of Thomas of Gaunt, from the Earl of Newport. This included the site of a residence of the Duke and Duchess of Somerset at Kingston Lacy.

The frontage of the Bankes Arms, looking eastwards.

Their late Victorian successor, Walter Ralph Bankes, was born in 1853. The Corfe Castle and Kingston Lacy Estates still extended to 30,000 acres. Though described as one the 'handsomest men of the age', Walter Bankes did not marry socialite Jenny Fraser until he was aged forty-four, in 1897. By then he was also prone to peculiar behaviour, such as setting off for America without telling anyone, which their daughter Viola put down to 'the disease which destroyed him at the early age of fifty-one'. He was particularly proud of describing himself as 'Lord High Admiral of the Purbeck Seas and last Mayor of Corfe Castle'. After his death, on 21 November 1904, the lands passed to his young son Ralph, born on 14 July 1902. He also left two daughters by wife Jenny and three older sons by his mistress.

CORFE CASTLE

Bankes Arms Hotel – 2000 (Rodney Legg)

The hotel was replaced by the present building in the 1930s and Mike Perry has been the landlord for the past decade. He played a leading role in organising the village Millennium Association's entertainments, culminating in a spectacular fireworks display, on Saturday 4 November 2000. Alison Wason and Mike Perry hosted a reception for the Twinning Association's contribution to millennium events. Founded in 1995, the association welcomed a record influx of French friends, with 34 coming from Pont Hebert.

Detailed view of the porch columns, plus pony, in 1970.

Ralph Bankes, who still owned an immense estate although its size had shrunk to 16,000 acres, died on 19 August 1981. He had been a virtual recluse in Kingston Lacy House since the death of his wife, Hilary, in 1966. It was expected that there might be surprises in his will, but not that son John Ralph Bankes would be virtually disinherited, with all the land and art treasures going to the National Trust. Executors handed over ownership on 19 August 1982. Valued rather conservatively, at £25 million, this was the Trust's greatest bequest, making media headlines for saving Corfe Castle for the nation.

CORFE CASTLE
Boar Mill – 1955

The pond on the Byle Brook, looking north-westwards over Boar Mill from the bridge on the hill in East Street, to the Plukenet Tower, King's Hall (right) and Keep of Corfe Castle. Nestling beneath the south-east side of Castle Hill, it is shown on a map of 1586 by Ralph Treswell though the present buildings date from the eighteenth and early nineteenth centuries. Like many Purbeck mills, clad in stone roof tiles, it maintained an ancient and characterful appearance. The leat, pond and sluiced weir contribute to the timeless setting.

Battrick's Bakery was is its local name. George Battrick was the baker and miller in mid-Victorian times and a century later, in the 1950s, the faggot-heated ovens were being stoked by Charles Battrick. Villagers praised gorse, or furze as it is known in Purbeck, for its contribution to the distinctive texture and quality of traditional country bread-making. Fourteen-year-old Edward Mullett began work in Boar Mill in 1926. He recalled at the end of the century that the winter's work of two men from Challow Farm was to go over the hill and cut a total of 2,000 wood faggots which the Rempstone Estate supplied to the bakery. These were long sticks cut from the hedgerows which supplemented the basic fuel supply of furze faggots from Corfe Common. Mr Mullett's main job was looking after the bakery's two horses: 'I can hear their wickering now as I would arrive to feed them at 7 am. I gave them a mix of furze, that had been through the chaff-cutter, with hay and oats that had been crushed at the mill. Once the horses were seen to I would help in the bakehouse. One of my jobs was to prepare the tins for the mixture to be dropped in. While the dough was proving I would put the rashers in the oven for breakfast. Once the smell of the freshly baked bread wafted up from the bakehouse, nearby villagers started to arrive, but there was no shop as such. We had our regular rounds, in and around the village, six days a week. I loaded the carts and harnessed the horses. Most loaves were one pound or two pounds in weight with a few of four pounds. Some people wanted them crusty or browned on the bottom, and we also made wholemeal and Hovis loaves.'

Boar Mill and pond, looking northwards from the bridge.

CORFE CASTLE
Boar Mill – 2000 (Rodney Legg)

Though the National Trust has sold some of the cottages which it inherited in Corfe Castle village, under the will of Ralph Bankes who died in 1981, it has also implemented a policy of acquiring properties that form an integral part of the scene. None qualified more than Boar Mill, which was purchased by the Trust in 1993, with the thought that it might provide an alternative access path for some of 170,000 people who visit the ruins of Corfe Castle each year. That became unnecessary when the Visitor Centre opened on the other side of Castle Hill but Boar Mill remains a key element of the setting.

The weir beside Boar Mill, southwards to cottages in East Street.

CORFE CASTLE
Corfe Castle and Castle Hill – 1892

The view eastwards, from West Hill, above the stone-slated roof of West Mill (centre, bottom), showing the bridge over the Church Knowle road with the village beyond, including the buildings around the Square and church tower (right). On top of Castle Hill is the Butavant Tower (centre) with the West Bailey and Keep behind it. To the left are North Tower and Inner Ward. On the other side, towards the village, the South Tower and ivy-clad South-West Gatehouse are followed four more towers.

Purbeck's world class monument has stood on Castle Hill for more than a thousand years. The strategic position is superb, commanding the passes on each side, and the visual splendour of the ruins is equal to anything in Europe. This side of the monument holds the clues to its origins. Herring-bone walling and windows of the Old Hall, a Norman Conquest period structure, stand on the site of the previous Saxon royal house and pre-date the rest of the ruins. This masonry can be found between the Butavant Tower and the South Tower on the south side of the West Bailey. It was at the entrance to this, at Edward's Gate which is now known as the South-West Gatehouse, that the boy-King Edward was assassinated by members of his step-mother's household in 978.

The great central Keep, an immense Norman structure, dates from 1095 to 1105. Despite demolitions it still stands, in part, to a height of 80 feet. It is one of the earliest mediaeval fortresses in Britain, with a general design and style well ahead of its time, built upon and otherwise surrounded by earlier eleventh-century walls which stood nearly 30 feet high on the outside. It survived King Stephen's failed siege to oust rebel baron Baldwin de Redvers in 1139. The West Bailey was re-fortified by King John in 1201 when he turned it into his state prison, for French captives, and in 1207 the Great Ditch was dug between the Keep and the vulnerable Outer Bailey, when John chose Corfe to hold his treasury. Military history ended with Civil War sieges, organised by heroic Lady Mary Bankes, which ended with treachery of Royalist officer Lieutenant-Colonel Thomas Pittman bringing about its surrender at 8 am on 27 February 1646. A few days later, on 4 March 1646, the House of Commons ordered the destruction of Corfe Castle. Even with tunnelling and explosives it was no easy task and the process of reducing it to ruins went on for months.

Corfe Castle and Nine Barrow Down as a train puffs into the cutting below East Hill.

CORFE CASTLE
Corfe Castle and Castle Hill – 1985 (Colin Graham)

Detail of the ruins on Castle Hill, from a higher point on West Hill, looking down from above the tree-line. The former West Mill became derelict and was demolished in about 1920. A chunk of masonry rolled down the hillside in the 1920s and destroyed my father's parked motor-cycle. Not that much more seems to be missing.

Civil War siege, as reconstructed by Phil Tebbutt, with the standard of Sir Walter Erle.

CORFE CASTLE

Castle and the Square – 1895

The view northwards from the church tower in the time of Rev. Eldon Surtees Bankes, the rector since 1854, to the almost new five-arch viaduct carrying the Swanage Railway over the Studland road. Beyond is a half-mile wide patch of white at Norden claypits. The public path around the south-eastern slopes of Castle Hill is also clearly visible in an age when most of the population did all routine movements on foot. The heart of Corfe Castle village is stone-roofed and already a time-warp in that despite Victorian expansionism and architectural flamboyance there is nothing from the nineteenth century to intrude in the foreground. The empty plinth of the Market Cross had yet to celebrate Queen Victoria's 'longest reign on record'.

Edwardian view from the tower, with the Market Cross firmly in place, in the postcard which the purchaser helpfully dated on 6 August 1906.

Behind the Market Cross, on the west side of the road into Corfe Castle, the eighteenth-century house is already a shop, with the sign being for baker and seedsman John George Luker. The main room has a delicate bay-window facing into the Square, with the figures beside a conventional window to the right of it. The doorway was then to the left of the bay-window. The other corner shop, to the east of the castle road, appears to be unoccupied. A seventeenth-century building, with a late nineteenth-century shopfront, it is the most recent renovation to be revealed by this photograph.

CORFE CASTLE

Castle and the Square – 1966

The view from the church tower, with the restored Market Cross having gone through its own diamond jubilee, as the Sixties went into full swing. It can be dated from the newest of the clutch of parked cars, which is a red mark-2 Ford Anglia, to the left of the Tuscan columns of the Greyhound Hotel. This vehicle, identified for me by Ollie Cassar, was introduced in August 1965.

J. G. Luker's shop has had its main window rebuilt, as a rectangular bay, and the other is now the door into the Castle Café. On either side of the Square the name Holland is writ large. Newsagent and entrepreneur E. O. Holland, with S. A. Walford, created a Model Village and Castle in the grounds behind

Castle past (left) and present, as seen from the Model Village.

the main shop (left), which looks across the deep-cut valley to the ruins of the real thing. It was completed in 1966. The newsagents is the nineteenth-century shop (centre) and the other store specialised in china and glass.

CORFE CASTLE
East Street, in a Victorian sketch – 1882 (Sir James Peile)

The artist Sir James Peile (1833-1906) provides us with another of those Corfe Castle views that remains totally unchanged. The month in 1882 was September. It is the classic view that the traveller enjoys, looking north-westwards down East Street to the Greyhound public house and ruins of Corfe Castle. Provision dealer George Cleall had his new shop, opened in 1881, in the eighteenth-century house immediately behind the projecting columns of the overhead room that match those of the Greyhound. The house next door is a century earlier and that behind the steps has a lozenge-shaped datestone for 1781.

The eighteenth-century house backing on to the churchyard, on the other side of the road, was converted into a Reading Room. James Riddle was remembered as its secretary by older villagers, whose parents visited each day during the Great War to read the latest news, hoping not to be personal participants in the tragedy.

Francis Newbery painted the Village Sign, facing the Greyhound, in 1927.

CORFE CASTLE
East Street – 2002 (Rodney Legg)

More than a century later, Cleall's Stores is still there (supplying me with my next roll of film, though the telephone number Corfe Castle 10 in my old notebook now sounds short on digits). Carol and John Elmes, in residence since 4 July 1994, installed their £500 metric scales on 4 January 2000. They go downstairs to the workplace at 6.30 am and half an hour later open the doors for the daily bread from Whites Bakery in Langton Matravers and Williams Bakery in Wool. Then the milkman arrives from Swanage. The shop eventually moved with the times, in 1999, and established the first video library between Wareham and Swanage. It is a 12-hour working day before Carol and John move on to their last chores and tidy-up before choosing a video and retiring upstairs.

In the foreground are the extending bedroom of number 27 East Street; number 29 is September Cottage; Merrilees, with the dormers is number 31; the next dormers are on number 33; numbers 35 and 37 have the steps. Across the road, the Reading Room now incorporates the tiny Box of Delight, and has been acquired by the National Trust to consolidate its management of the Square. In my case the personal delight was a double cornet of stem-ginger ice cream but for the queue of ladies it was chocolate, chocolate and chocolate.

Frontage of the Greyhound Hotel, under a veranda, in 1928, with the Roadster probably being photographer Edwin Dodshon's motor car.

CORFE CASTLE
Greyhound Hotel, in a water-colour issued as a postcard – 1903

The Greyhound Hotel looking north-eastwards towards East Hill, as it was in the time of Miss Mary Desallioud. Charles Desallioud was the landlord half a century earlier. Byron Cooksley followed before the Great War. Two seventeenth-century houses in the Square were merged into a single dwelling by 'I. C.' for Joshua Churchill whose datestone for 1733 is set under the front window above one of the two sets of three elegant Tuscan columns. These were erected across the pavement to support projecting rooms above. This western porch is still open, as built, but two of the three eastern columns have been encased in nineteenth-century brickwork (right) causing the footway to be diverted around the front.

Towards the rear, 40 feet back from the road, a late-seventeenth-century date is indicated by the nature of the building materials. There is reused mediaeval ashlar, and a thirteenth-century coping stone in the stables, identical to one that is still in place in Corfe Castle. Much of the village was refurbished from its ruins.

Tuscan columns supporting the porch, with a 1733 datestone (centre, top).

CORFE CASTLE
Greyhound Hotel – 2000 (Rodney Legg)

The Greyhound Hotel looked almost identical at the end of the century except for the inevitable parked cars. There is a lead Sun Insurance Company insurance mark, number 19420, under the left-hand eaves of the western porch. Other details are also reassuringly similar, including the window frames, and though one laments the emulsion painting of stone buildings, white walls were traditional as the visual indicator of a public house. Maroon woodwork in Purbeck and east Dorset is generally the mark of Bankes Estate ownership, since turned into a fine art by the National Trust, but here it coincides with the livery of brewers Whitbread and Company.

Old-master style for a rigid pose on the Greyhound sign, also showing the datestone (bottom left).

CORFE CASTLE
The Square – 1905

The Square, looking southwards from the Market Cross to the eighteenth-century Town House and its first-floor Mayor's robing room, and tower of the parish church of Saint Edward, King and Martyr. The steps of the ancient Market Cross were used as a plinth for the erection of a replacement to celebrate Queen Victoria's diamond jubilee in 1897. On the east side is the Town Pump, above St Edward's Well, which may be the very spot where the corpse of the assassinated Saxon youth was hidden on 18 March 978, before burial in a marsh. The acidic peat may have preserved 'the holy King's body' as it was claimed to be uncorrupted when moved from Wareham to Shaftesbury Abbey by Ealdorman Aelfhere in 980.

The Square, looking westwards to the National Trust shop, as villagers celebrate Queen Elizabeth's golden jubilee in June 2002 with 'the best display in Purbeck'.

King John granted Corfe a weekly Saturday market in 1215 and Henry III added a Thursday market in 1248. By custom in 1381 it was required that any merchant obtaining fish from the Royal Warren had to offer it first for sale for an hour at 'the Cross of Corfe'. This was to give residents a chance of buying food before it was removed from the Isle of Purbeck. The Cross was also used for religious services on high days and holidays and for declaring election results. It was demolished during the Reformation and the base used for erecting a pillory. This was still there in 1585, with stocks nearby, and the latter were last used in about 1860. The new Cross was unveiled by Rev. Eldon Surtees Bankes, rector of Corfe, on St Edward's Day, also marking the Queen's accession, a year after the jubilee, on 20 June 1898. That was also an important year for the rector who was appointed Canon Residentiary of Salisbury.

CORFE CASTLE
The Square – 1928 (Edwin Dodshon)

I was going to use my present-day equivalent of the above shot, but it is identical to this one by Bournemouth amateur photographer Edwin Dodshon, except that mine lacks the 1926-registered Roadster, PR 2825, parked in West Street outside Mrs E. Sheasby's Castle Cafe and Tea Gardens. 'It's sporty enough to have been the doctor's,' a villager told me, in a reference to Dr Godfrey Dru Drury who became a living legend for having brought the first De Dion Bouton to Corfe in 1910. More likely, however, it was Mr Dodshon's own motor car, as it also appears around the corner in a shot of the Greyhound. Professionally, Dodshon was a Bournemouth solicitor, with offices in Christchurch Road.

Town Pump, with lead spout and the borough's ancient seal, above St Edward's Well beside the Market Cross.

The refreshment rooms are now the National Trust shop and the Town House is the Post Office, though with a very discrete sign which was hidden in my picture by the shaft of the cross. Historians call this the Market Place but to villagers it is the Square.

CORFE CASTLE
Station Road – 1905

Visitors to Corfe Castle, arriving by train, had a perfect view of the castle ruins, north-westwards across the valley. Its Keep and Outer Bailey were perfectly visible, in a mediaeval panorama virtually uninterrupted by later architecture, extending round Castle Hill to the far towers and West Hill beyond. This was built as a private road, by the railway builders in 1885, as is proved by a cast-iron boundary marker set in the ground beside the Bankes Arms fence. 'L & S. W. Ry Co' it reads, for the London and South Western Railway Company.

The flock of pure-bred Dorset Downs, with an accompanying cart of hay, are a reminder that this was still sheep country. The principal downland farmers on the Purbeck Hills were the Smiths. Herbert and Samuel Smith were at Rollington, and John Smith at Ailwood, and Seth Smith at Brenscombe, or Brinscombe as it was always pronounced. The biggest flock was that of Samuel James Smith, who had 225 breeding ewes and 80 ewe hoggets at the end of the Great War. He had three rams, supplied by Joseph Osmond Symes, from Swyre. On the other side of the village, on the limestone ridge, Henry Legg had a similar flock at Blashenwell Farm and John Stevens twice the number at Eastington.

Railway company boundary marker beside the Bankes Arms Hotel.

CORFE CASTLE
Station Road – 2002

A view at Corfe Castle that no one would now photograph. It is still there, but completely blocked, by the trees around the beer garden of the Bankes Arms Hotel. Glance to the right, however, and the single break in the jungle canopy yields a glimpse of the north end of Corfe Castle Station and the line from the signal to the cutting on East Hill. At the other end of the beer garden the railway company's iron marker stands beside the fence.

Mainline 4-6-2 Merchant Navy class locomotive 35027 Port Line, *built at Eastleigh in 1949, in steam at Corfe Castle Station in 2002.*

35027 Port Line *pulling out of Corfe Castle, towards Norden, in the only available view from the Bankes Arms beer garden in 2002.*

CORFE CASTLE
West Mill – 1907

Edwardian idyll of the rustic mill beside the Corfe River, lying below Castle Hill, immediately downstream from the bridge carrying the lane to Church Knowle. This intimate view is westwards across the stepping stones. These provided a direct route into the village, following Oliver Vye's Lane beside the Wicken Stream, on the other side of the road. The stone-roofed thirteenth-century buildings ceased to be a mill in 1790 and were converted to cottages. Winifred Stockley was born here in 1907. The cottages were home to the large family of clay-worker Walter Stockley and his wife Ida.

West Mill shortly before 1900, in another photograph from the east side of the Corfe River, before that part of the setting was engulfed by roadside trees.

CORFE CASTLE
West Mill – 2002 (Rodney Legg)

The cottages at West Mill gradually fell into disrepair and were demolished in about 1920. Clearance was never completed, however, and a stone-walled channel remains. In the surviving chunk of the east wall is a brick-arched recess in which the water-wheel turned. These and other footings were cleared of scrub by the National Trust and excavated in 1997. The single unaltered part of the setting are the steps into the river which are surmounted by a 6 feet by 4 feet flagstone. Most of the stepping stones have been displaced though some of the originals survive. National Trust archaeologists Nancy Grace and Pete Mould are considering more work to consolidate the remains.

The Stockleys were to be the last family to live in West Mill, ending seven centuries of continuous habitation, having finally tired of recurrent floods, leaking roofs and ivy-clad chimneys. Walter's health was too poor to enable him to do much about their situation and he died at the age of fifty-four. Ida found herself bringing up their eight children without any help. One of them, Winifred Stockley who was born at West Mill in 1907, recalled that during floods they had to clamber out of an upstairs window, on to the bank at the back of the house, in order to go to school. Among other excitements were sheep-dipping in the river and the occasional splash and shout as someone fell into the river from the stepping stones. The agent for the Bankes Estate – at a time when it was in limbo with owner Ralph Bankes progressing from Eton to Magdalen College in Oxford – reluctantly agreed that the building was 'uninhabitable'. He moved the Stockleys up into Corfe Castle, to No 10 West Street, where Ida Stockley lived for the rest of her life. Grannie Stockley, as she became known to the village, died at the age of ninety-six in 1982. Her descendants are still living in Corfe.

The footings of West Mill, after excavation in 1997, with the mill-wheel channel showing as a dark hole.

CORFE CASTLE

West Street – 1900

Northwards from 1741-dated Farthing Cottage (left), near the south end of what used to be the main mediaeval road into Corfe Castle, from the quarrylands and Kingston. Other eighteenth-century cottages stand on both sides of West Street. April Cottage (right) is a detached thatched building. Cottages on the other side of the road, behind the rustic cart-shed, comprise a range of five small dwellings with a larger one adjoining on the end. Another cottage stands behind. Further along the street, on the right, is Becky Webber Cottage beside the footpath into Webber's Close.

The view in an Edwardian postcard, showing the cart-shed gone.

The swirling serifs of the datestone over the doorway into Farthing Cottage (No 104 West Street) has an 'H' above as the initial of the family name and 'E' and 'N' for his and her personal names. It is a single storey building with an attic floor which has dormer windows with pent roofs. The Royal Commission on Historical Monuments identifies 'a wall-anchor of millrind shape'.

CORFE CASTLE

West Street – 2002 (Rodney Legg)

The first casualty in the view was the cart-shed. Edwardian postcards show that it had gone by 1905 and site remains grassed over. The present view, from the entrance to Hillside which is opposite Springwood, shows a mass of foliage obscuring Farthing Cottage, the modern cottage beside it, and the older range of cottages behind of numbers 98 through to 90 West Street.

Smartly-tooled script on the datestone in Farthing Cottage.

Further along the street, beyond Webber's Close, at the age of fifty-eight, Michael Bond achieved one of Corfe Castle's first honourable moments since it lost its Members of Parliament and Mayor as 'the rottenest borough in the land'. At home in Furzeman's House on 6 April 2000, wife Anne prepared for 38 guests as he put on eighteenth-century court dress of 'stockings (actually tights), knee breeches, velvet waistcoat, cutaway tail-coat' but sans both sword and tricorn hat. Nine-year-old Alexander Bond looked on as his father 'made my declaration' by reading his oath of office as High Sheriff of Dorset for millennium year. It is 'the oldest secular appointment in the country after the sovereign' he tells us in *Corfe Castle 2000: A diary of the village*. That Thursday was indeed 'a lovely bright sunny day'. I was out taking blue-sky photographs.

Farthing Cottage shows that size is not everything.

CREECH

Creech Grange – 1857 (John Pouncy)

North side, with gardener in 1911, looking towards the Purbeck Hills.

The first of Dorset's landscape photographers, John Pouncy of Dorchester also pioneered the technique of lithograph printing, publishing his *Dorsetshire Illustrated* in 1857. Its exceedingly rare volumes represent the first coffee-table photographic books in the land: 'The Detail and Touch of Nature faithfully reproduced by a New Process on Stone, by which views are rendered Truthful, Artistic, and Durable.' Durable is also the word that applies to Creech Grange, the east front of which Pouncy photographed, looking westwards to West Creech Hill. It was built by Sir Oliver Lawrence on former Bindon Abbey lands, in about 1545, and extended on the north side in about 1600. The Lawrence shields-of-arms are on panels in the barrel-vaulted roof, and also carved in the porch and above a door, in Steeple parish church on the other side of the Purbeck Hills. The 1616-dated heraldry depicts the crests of Lawrence quartering Washington's stars and stripes (correctly called 'bars and mullets'). The initials 'D.L.E.' were for Edward Lawrence. This Dorset connection assumed its significance when descendant George Washington was proclaimed first President of the 'United States of America' as the Congress of British Provinces styled themselves, in revolt, on 9 September 1776 after having declared 'free, sovereign and independent nationhood' on 4 July 1776. Washington's elder half-brother was named Lawrence.

The other notable family name in these parts is that of Bond of Bond Street and there is an Old Bond Street at Creech to remind us of the fact. Ian Fleming, though giving his James a Scottish pedigree, admitted the Dorset ancestry. Nathaniel Bond arrived at Creech in 1691 and Rev. Nathaniel Bond was in residence when Walter Pouncy visited with his tripod.

CREECH

Creech Grange – 2002 (Rodney Legg)

South front, seen from across the lawn in 1997, in the last of the light before a thunderstorm breaks.

Visibly only the trees are different. The notable thing that happened at Creech Grange in the twentieth-century was the end of the era of the Bonds. In 1981, after the death of Lieutenant-Colonel Ashley Bond, the house was bought by Parkstone-born football club owner Norman Hayward. His wife Pat, who established the first cancer charity shop in Britain, in Wareham, died in 1992. Norman Hayward, helped by daughters Lorraine and Michelle, carried on her work. He bought St Michael's Church at Steeple to preserve it for the parish after the building had been declared redundant. Creech, or Grange as the Victorians used to refer to it, also has its own private chapel, tucked away in the trees behind the house.

East Burton, Dorset.

EAST BURTON
East Burton Dairy – 1910

As a hamlet of Winfrith Newburgh parish, the earliest documentary mention of East Burton was in 1210, but it is now incorporated into Wool parish. The picture dates from the time when William White was being succeeded at 115-acre Burton Dairy by farmer John Keynes whose dairyman was William Pitman. The lane from the roadside cob and thatch Seven Stars hostelry into Wool crossed the stream from Winfrith Heath at a ford.

This view north-eastwards into Water Meadow Road, to Burton Farm and Burton Dairy House (centre), also shows the gable-end of thatched Snipe Cottage (right). East Burton was a hamlet - originally a tithing - of Winfrith Newburgh parish. Half a mile west of Wool Station, the Southampton and Dorchester Railway was built across meadows at East Burton in 1846, by engineer Captain William Moorsom. A level-crossing was provided on the lane south to 'the new Protestant chapel' consecrated on 7 September 1840.

East Burton Dairy House after being gutted by fire in 1968.

Shorn-sheep, led by shepherd Richard Marriott from East Burton Dairy, to a pasture on the other side of the railway line.

EAST BURTON
East Burton Dairy – 2002 (Rodney Legg)

Since transferred, administratively, from Winfrith Newburgh to Wool parish, it has been visually all-change in this view. First the stream was put into a culvert. The road (foreground, left to right) leads from a very different Seven Stars – now a modern roadhouse set back on a rise – into what has become a suburb of Wool. The photograph is from Colts Close and the road towards the railway level-crossing.

East Burton Dairy House, destroyed by fire, was pictured by me as a single-storey brick shell in 1968. It is identifiable from its porch and eastern chimney-stack. Though brick-built, and dated by the Royal Commission on Historical Monuments as being from the nineteenth century date, farmer Geoffrey Hyde points out that it had stone foundations centuries older, and other earlier features revealed by the fire. 'I was away that winter,' he told me. 'Otherwise I would not have let the estate clear it away. It should have been rebuilt.' Snipe Cottage has survived but in summer disappears behind the trees.

Holme Lane, Wareham. 1501
Hills & Rownays Series.

EAST HOLME
Holme Lane – 1912

The attractive road on the south side of the Frome meadows, from Stoborough to Wool, is seen on a straight section near the bridge over the Swanage Railway. The view is westwards, with Holme Lane Plantation to the right and similar woods to the left hiding Squirrel's Cottages. Pine trees and banks of ponticum rhododendrons are the principal vegetation.

My father, Ted Legg who was born in Bournemouth in 1902, enjoyed riding along here in the 1920s. He had a motor-cycle with sidecar combination, and recalled splashing through a succession of fords. His diary for 23 May 1937 records a dramatic thunderstorm over Holme Lane. Its fords have since been bridged but one survives in East Holme village.

Jack Abbott, who began clay-mining in 1937, on the work-face below Holme Lane in 1973.

EAST HOLME
Holme Lane – 2002 (Rodney Legg)

The road looks much the same, still tunnelled though woodland, though there are now more oak trees and fewer pines. The lorry, in the blue livery of ECC Ball Clays, is carrying a full load eastwards to Furzebrook Works, from an open pit beside the site of Squirrel's Cottages in the woods to the left. Here, before the increasingly complexity of health and safety regulations brought an end to underground workings, Colin Graham and I went down an Adit-type mine in 1973. It was beside danger flag number 41 of the Lulworth and East Holme Ranges.

I am therefore one of the few people who can claim to have stood beneath this view. The headgear looked like the set for a John Ford western, and was the domain of a character to match, namely Hubert Coffin. Iron arch-girders, put in place in 1965, clad a 22-inch gauge railway down a steep incline (gradient 1 in 3.5) down to the working floor 60 feet below. We followed the railway, stepping aside in alcoves for trucks to pass, to a work-face 300 yards away. Here the 'lens' of clay was 'in the pink' with its usual grey tinted by iron-staining. Jack Abbott was cutting into it with pneumatic drills. His younger mate, Trevor Seager, loaded the trucks. One danger, explosive methane, was rare in clay seams with their absence of lignitic material, but might come from the decaying timbers of older workings. Water seepage, however, was a real and constant risk, liable to break-

The ford at East Holme during momentary seasonal weather in the wet summer of 2002.

through from a seepage to 200 gallons a minute. Moss was advised as a natural filter for blocking weak spots but in Purbeck heather was found to be better and also made good footings for roadways. In 1973 it was still proving more efficient than fabric fillers. Ball clay is a constantly pure rock which handles perfectly, without mess or dust, with the result that the air was fresh and comfortably cool at a constant temperature between 50 to 55 degrees Fahrenheit. Unlike some of the visitors I suffered no claustrophobia. 'You start work on Monday, then,' Hubert said as I returned to the top.

EAST LULWORTH
Cockles and Littlemore – 1901

Ivy on tile-clad walls at thatched Littlemore Cottage (left) and numbers 18 and 19 East Lulworth (right) at Cockles, looking northwards beside the stream from Water Barrows. Out of the picture, further to the right, are number 20 and gritty heath-stone-walled Cockles Cottage, comprising numbers 21 and 22. Cockles Cottage is the oldest of the cluster, dating back to the seventeenth century, with the other buildings in this thatched corner spanning the next 200 years. It looks like a rural backwater that has been here for ever but the expansion of East Lulworth village, eastwards into pastures won from the heath, was caused by one of Dorset's parkland clearances. Feudal masters in this case were the Welds, one

Old School House was the Protestant National School.

of the most powerful Catholic families in the land, whose Roman Catholic church was the first erected in England since the Reformation, disguised as a temple and hidden on instructions from George III, behind Lulworth Castle.

Unfashionable formal gardens were replaced by a sprawling landscaped park and the estate workers were moved to a new East Lulworth out of sight behind a wall and trees. Cockles becomes School Lane (far left) with two elementary schools provided in Victorian times. The usual Purbeck sectarian divide was between Church and Chapel; here the split was between Anglican and Catholic. The former had an 1840-built National School for 80 children (average attendance 50) with Mrs Ann Trent as the mistress in the 1890s. Further along the road, beneath an ancient oak which it was a rite of passage for the boys to climb, was the 1855-built St Mary's Catholic School for 100 children (average attendance 40, later swelled by arrivals from Lulworth Camp and West Lulworth). Its mistress was Miss Ellen Fanning. Nuns from St Mary's House, around the next corner beside Manor Cottage, taught the next generation.

EAST LULWORTH
Cockles and Littlemore – 2002 (Rodney Legg)

The backwater has been preserved by two accidents of history. There are still roads in both directions beside Littlemore Cottage but East Lulworth's through-road as chosen by the highway authority is via the Weld Arms, following the park wall between the entrance and exit gates to Lulworth Castle. In the other direction, up the sandy track and behind Elm Tree House, the War Department provided its alternative road for military vehicles to by-pass the community. Beyond are the Lulworth Ranges.

The Angelus bell is no longer tolled at St Mary's Catholic School.

Elm Tree House, a Victorian villa, is the home of Stephen and Richard Levett. On the other side of the Army's road, this section of the tank gunnery ranges is permanently out-of-bounds, including Bronze Age burial mounds at Water Barrows, Ferny Barrows and on Boat Knoll.

EAST LULWORTH
Lulworth Castle – 1929

Fire, apparently from 'fused electric wire' on the top floor, took hold and raged through the Lulworth Castle home of the Weld family on 29 August 1929. Firemen, estate workers and villagers struggled through the afternoon to save antiques, paintings and movable items of furniture. Salvaged items accumulated in great piles on each side of the building, with this view looking eastwards, to the rear steps of the west frontage, but many priceless historical relics were destroyed, including the elaborate King's Room and its bed. This had been made for George III. Lulworth also had the close associations for his son. Maria Anne Smythe, widow of Edward Weld and then Thomas Fitzherbert, illegally married George IV.

Lulworth Castle was reduced to a gutted shell. The family's leading scholar was Herbert Weld, South African correspondent of the *Morning Post* during the Boer War, who became an eminent archaeologist and brought back thousands of inscribed tablets and finds from Iraq in 1922. He visited Thomas Hardy at Max Gate, Dorchester, on 19 September 1927, and had the distinction of featuring in the last entry the author made in his personal notebook, shortly before he died. Herbert Weld expressed relief that most of his priceless antiquities were safely in the Ashmolean Museum and other national collections. The Luttrell Psalter, now in the British Museum, had already been removed from the castle.

The King's Bed at Lulworth Castle was destroyed in the fire on 29 August 1929.

EAST LULWORTH
Lulworth Castle – 1995 (Rodney Legg)

The west side of Lulworth Castle following restoration by English Heritage as an empty but accessible shell. Work started after the ruin had been taken into guardianship by the Directorate of Ancient Monuments and Historic Buildings in 1981.

Herbert Weld died in 1935. The estate was inherited by his first cousin once removed. Colonel Sir Joseph Weld, as wartime staff officer to Lord Louis Mountbatten, escorted Lady Edwina Mountbatten on a dangerous mission after D-Day in which she descended on field hospitals like a latter-day Florence Nightingale. Their closest call came as German flak riddled the borrowed

The Saloon at Lulworth Castle, with its fine ceiling, before the fire of 1929.

Avro Anson, taking out one of its two engines, with one of the party hit in the face. The New Zealand pilot 'just managed to hedge-hop back over our lines, and the journey had to be completed by jeep.' What impressed everyone was that as a consummate socialite Edwina Mountbatten made 'quick repairs to her make-up' and breezed into a surgery ward exuding calm and confidence: 'She put her all into every performance - and was perfection.' Sir Joseph Weld died in 1992 and his son Wilfrid Weld, born in 1934, heads the family into the new millennium, with their home now being Lulworth Castle House.

FURZEBROOK

The Blue Pool – 1935

The best known of Purbeck's abandoned claypits, the Blue Pool at Furzebrook, was cut by Watts, Hatherley and Burns of Newton Abbot in about 1846. The boys who removed the overburden of heathland sand were paid 12 shillings a week and given a hot meal each day. Their wheelbarrows, called rubblers, were pushed up planks to the top of the pit and spoil heaps gathered beyond. A railway was laid across the heath, to a wharf on the tidal River Frome at Ridge, and the ball clay was supplied by sea and canal to Royal Worcester, Minton, Wedgwood and other leading pottery manufacturers of the day. Walter

The sandy southern shore of the Blue Pool, looking eastwards to the biggest spoil heap, in 1936.

Pike bought the Blue Pool in 1874. By the end of the century the lunar landscape of pits and spoils heaps, reached by tentacles of steam-operated tramways, had moved on to Cotness and Creech. They then extended westwards to Povington Heath. By then, in 1935, visitors were visiting the Blue Pool to admire its bright colours and tranquil setting. This view, south-eastwards, is to the wood on Knowle Hill.

T. T. Barnard of Furzebrook House had the inspired idea of turning it into a commercial beauty spot. The vivid and ever-changing turquoise and blue colour of the pool is caused by diffracted light passing through the mineral particles of clay that are permanently suspended in the water. Miss J. S. Barnard, the present owner of the Blue Pool, pointed out to me in November 1972 that to the surprise of visitors this blueness is stronger on overcast days, when there is no sunlight reflected off the surface of the lake. The water is also dead. The high concentration of minerals and an absence of oxygen prevents decomposition and for this reason the pool has no vegetable or animal life. Three acres of water are surrounded by 25 acres of sandy slopes covered by woodland, furze and heather.

FURZEBROOK

The Blue Pool – 1999 (Rodney Legg)

Woodland now predominates in the immediate vicinity of the Blue Pool, making it increasingly difficult to replicate the original open views, though the white sands of the south-eastern corner can still be glimpsed from the perimeter path. Other flooded pits have become water-lily lakes. Well over a century after it was abandoned, and flooded, silt remains in suspension in the Blue Pool and its colour seems to be as strong as ever.

South-westwards, to the 634-feet high summit of Creech Barrow Hill, in 1959.

Walter Pike's business absorbed his local rivals as it grew into Pike Brothers, Fayle and Company, which is now absorbed into the giant combine English China Clays. That causes confusion but does not affect the status of the Purbeck product. It it is ball clay – not china clay – and took its name from the 'tubal' spade which was used in the cutting.

GOLDEN BOWL

Encombe House, in a pen-and-wash sketch − 1853 (C. M. Colvile)

The lake-side frontage of Encombe House, looking north-eastwards, into the romantically named Golden Bowl. The pleasantly simple south-facing frontage was completed by William Morton Pitt in 1770. It lies at the heart of a circular valley below Swyre Head, which at 666 feet above sea level is the highest hill in Purbeck, with the overflow from the lake trickling through the wooded South Gwyle hollow and falling into the sea with a waterfall at Freshwater. The ring of hills protect the Golden Bowl from the drawbacks of a location only 1,000 yards inland from windswept ledges and cliffs.

Encombe House at the centre of the Golden Bowl.

William Morton Pitt sold Encombe in 1807 to John Scott, 1st Earl of Eldon, who was Lord High Chancellor of England from 1801, almost continuously, to 1827. 'Almost the ideal of manly beauty,' to admirers, in cabinet he was reluctant and reactionary when it came to resisting reforms. Eldon was the last bastion of power against extending voting rights, revising Parliamentary boundaries, and emancipating Roman Catholics. He famously prevented the poet Shelley from having custody of his children. Relaxing at home he was never happier 'than when among the birds at Encombe' but was seldom much of a threat to them as he could 'kill nothing but time'. He erected a 40-feet Egyptian style obelisk as a monument to his brother Sir William Scott, 1st Baron Stowell, who was a friend of Dr Johnson and the pre-eminent draughtsman of international maritime law. Lord Chancellor Eldon's favourite viewpoint is marked by Eldon Seat, the first stone of which was laid by Lady Elizabeth Repton in 1835. Beside it is a memorial to Pincher, the late Lord Eldon's last dog, who outlived his master by two years and died in 1840.

GOLDEN BOWL

Encombe House − 1969

The house remained the Scott family home for the whole of the twentieth century but the title of the Earl of Eldon and his heir, Viscount Encombe, moved inland to Stowell Park, Gloucestershire, and Wimbledon suburbia. The second son of the 3rd Earl of Eldon was the diplomat the Honourable Sir Ernest Stowell Scott. Family lands extended across Purbeck from coast to coast, from the English Channel to Poole Harbour, including claypits operated by English China Clays. Much of the heathland, across the Arne peninsula, was leased and then sold to the Royal Society for the Protection of Birds. By 2002, Encombe itself was on the market, as one of the most desirable country houses in the land with 2,000 of its best acres.

Eldon Seat, below Swyre Head, marks Lord Chancellor Eldon's favourite view.

HERSTON

Jubilee Road – 1892

The rutted path-like road across the foreground (left to right) is Bell Street and the view is westwards into Jubilee Road which was named in 1887 by contractor and developer George Burt to celebrate the fiftieth year of Queen Victoria's reign. Henry Masterman and Edmund Woodrow, in Jubilee Terrace, were the local shoe-makers and cobblers. Bell Street took its name from irascible rector Rev. Andrew Bell, an old India hand who pioneered the 'Madras System' of education in which older children taught the younger ones.

Rose Cottage is still part of the view.

Herston was still a distinct hamlet but the building line was approaching from nearby Swanage. Up the slope, to the left, the road led into the quarrylands beside the Priests Way which had its origins in the Middle Ages when Swanage was a chapelry of the Norman church at Worth Matravers. Stone merchants Thomas Stevens and Sons operated the main workings. Along the street to the right, Herston Church of England School was built in 1855 for 120 children, and Miss Mary Fright was the mistress. In the hamlet, a mile west of Swanage, Frederick Billett and Edward Courtney were the blacksmiths, and William Farwell the licensee of the Globe Inn at the north end of Bell Street. Baker Jon Honebon offered 'whole-meal bread and self-raising flour' and specialised as a 'confectioner, pastrycook, fancy bread and biscuit maker'. On the main road, Thomas Stockley was the shopkeeper, Joseph George Harris the grocer, and Henry Haysom the landlord at the Royal Oak, opposite Washpond Lane. King and Son were water mineral manufacturers. Seth Marshfield was the principal farmer and John Parsons the dairyman.

HERSTON

Jubilee Road – 2001 (Rodney Legg)

The modern view is from Shirley Close into Jubilee Road, to a just visible Rose Cottage (left), with The Nook and Forget-me-not behind the trees. The latter was sold to Henry Coffin by George Burt, contractor and entrepreneur, who Thomas Hardy described as 'the King of Swanage'. Burt told Coffin he had a bargain that he would regret and added: 'When you sell it, don't forget me.' Typical of properties on the Burt Estate it had been provided with redundant cannon-bollards from London streets. 'St James's Clerkenwell' and 'St Anne' are the parish names cast in iron on either side of the garden gate.

Cannon bollards, removed from London streets, as gate-posts in Jubilee Road.

Ken Dodd, my informant from No. 51 Bell Street - apparently no relation to the comedian - told me that The Nook was the oldest building, traditionally said to have been a single-storey hunting lodge, with inglenook fireplace and baking oven. Victoria Terrace is beyond and the garage of Milton to the right. Down the street the school survives as Swanage St Mark's Church of England First School and its next-door 1867-dated Reading Room is St Mark's pre-school.

KIMMERIDGE

Clavell Tower – 1900

A folly on Hen Cliff, the Clavell Tower is seen in use as a Coastguard lookout, in a view north-westwards over Kimmeridge Bay to foothills of Tyneham Cap. It is 40-feet high and stands on the 120-feet contour. Though on a relatively lowly position it is at the centre of the view along the seaboard from Gad Cliff to St Alban's Head. Inland, rising to 666 feet, Swyre Head is the highest point in the Isle of Purbeck. It used to be assumed that the Clavell Tower dated from the 1820s, until Major John Mansel of Smedmore House told me he had found its building bills, dated 1831, in the estate archives. The builder was Rev. John Richards who assumed the Clavell name of the Kimmeridge gentry on inheriting the estate

Smedmore House is a mile inland from the tower.

in 1817. A circular three-storey structure, it is surrounded by a colonnade, with brick and stone rubble faced with stucco and ashlar. Several old cannon were placed around the flagpole, each set in the ground at an angle, to hold its stays.

Apart from being used by the Coastguard service, as a conspicuous seamark it soon proved of value, saving at least one crew in peril from foundering on the treacherous Kimmeridge Ledges. The chief officer, John Macgillicuddy, lived in the Coastguard Station to the north and had five men under his command. During the Great War they were led by Percy Pearson. Eliza Bright Nicholls, the daughter of a George Nicholls, a Cornish Coastguard stationed at Kimmeridge in the 1850s, became the girl friend of young architect and author Thomas Hardy. The Clavell Tower had its romantic associations for Hardy. It features in the shadowy background to the sketch of a coastal couple drawn for his 'She, to Him' series of *Wessex Poems*. Eliza and Thomas re-visited Kimmeridge on 3 September 1863.

KIMMERIDGE

Clavell Tower – 2000 (Rodney Legg)

By the 1930s, the Coastguards gone, the Clavell Tower had been gutted by fire. It remains an empty shell which by the end of the millennium was causing concern. Hen Cliff has gradually eroded and is now only 6 feet away. If the sea comes any closer the structure will be doomed. The situation will have become so precarious, legally as well as physically, that health and safety regulations will prevent any further remedial work. The only solution is for it to be taken down stone by stone and rebuilt a safe distance to the east.

Thriller writer P. D. James changed its colour and used it as the setting for *The Black Tower* in 1975. The gist of the story is that a care-home for the disabled is run by a sinister figure who meets his fate in the Clavell Tower where he is walled up and left to die. She now champions the cause of saving the monument: 'It's not sinister in real life, but its fate, in falling over the cliff, has a touch of melancholy.'

The Clavell Tower at sunset from its landward side.

139 Kimmeridge P.O.

KIMMERIDGE

Post Office – 1930

The Post Office, looking north-westwards to the ridge west of Smedmore Hill, in the time of shopkeeper Frederick Henry Cooper (telephone Kimmeridge 1). His predecessors, a century earlier, were a clan of incorrigible smugglers, with Reuben Cooper (aged twenty) being fined £100 in 1821 and Charles Cooper (twenty-seven) imprisoned for six months at Dorchester in 1840. His behaviour, according to the gaol register, was 'disorderly'. When the time came to hang-up the grappling hooks and casks these found their way to the Dorset County Museum.

1848 date on the stone above the porch and an invisible doorway to No. 24 Kimmeridge.

An 1848 datestone can be seen above the arched opening into the thatched porch. Next-door there are shutters on the downstairs windows. The picture has been taken from the public path that used to run through the playground of what was the 1866-built National School for Promoting the Education of the Poor in the Principles of the Established Church. Wonderfully snappy title – no wonder they were known simply as National Schools – these were education classes for Anglicans. At Kimmeridge the school catered for 80 children, with 60 being the average attendance, but had peaks with the arrival of labourers mining 'blackstone' shale from the cliffs. It was hauled along tramways to piers beside the bay for shipment to Wareham and Weymouth. There a wide variety of coal-tar products was extracted including naphtha for lighting the streets of Paris. Kimmeridge Bay also hosted the Coastguard service, until after the Great War, when Mrs Charlotte Millard was the mistress at the Elementary School. The population of 117 could only barely justify its continuation.

KIMMERIDGE

Nos. 24 and 25 Kimmeridge – 2002 (Rodney Legg)

The Elementary School is now the Old School House. The public path has been diverted northwards via the Village Hall and a scraggy hedge has replaced the neat stone walls. These and a builder's van contrived to reduce any closer attempt at a comparative photograph to a composition of foliage and steel. The porch with the 1848 date-stone hides behind another mass of vegetation, making for a delightful front garden, but again blocking comparison. The Post Office is number 24 Kimmeridge with numbers 25 and 26 next-door. This street forms the stem of a 'T' with the Kimmeridge Farmhouse, the parish church – historic dedication unknown – and Old Parsonage on the bar at the top.

The present Post Office offers refreshments.

Between them, in the right-hand corner, is the current Post Office which also presents a thatched profile. Its chances of survival have been enhanced by diversification into tea-rooms and provision of a large car-park with children's swings on the grass across the road. I've seen it doing brisk business in January. As a magnet for walkers it has no local competition as Kimmeridge lost its New Inn in the nineteenth century.

KINGSTON HILL
Scoles Farm – 1925

The view north-westwards of the oldest inhabited building in Corfe Castle parish, dating from 1300 or earlier, between Corfe Common and Kingston. Parts of a small hall-house of that date, including a mullioned window, are incorporated in the outbuildings. These are full of original features, such as a blocked chamfered doorway and a buttery-hatch, with the walls rebuilt with buttresses and a rare series of bee-boles. There was also an ancient chapel to the west. This site, which takes its name from William de Scovill in 1244, was at a crossroads of old tracks between Corfe Castle and marble workings on the ridge from Kingston towards Langton Matravers. The present house is a smart seventeenth-century building.

Unchanged for centuries, Scoles Farm was sketched by Alfred Dawson in 1882.

KINGSTON HILL
Scoles Manor – 1988

Gentrification at Scoles Farm, with the arrival of Belinda and Peter Bell in 1988, was accompanied by the revival of its mediaeval credentials. Scoles Manor also retains a smallholding look with calves, black Sumatra game-fowl and India runner ducks, in a scene all the more bizarre for the ostriches on the other side of the farm fence. The Bells have converted the barns into self-catering accommodation. A fuller picture of family life emerges from the wonderful *Corfe Castle 2000: Diary of a Village*. The grown-up children are Andrew, Carrie, Liz and Will. We are told that at 4.30 am on 4 June 2000 first son Andrew was completing their web-site (www.scoles.co.uk). Second son Will was in the middle of his finals at Oxford.

It was a particular milestone for the building that has been in continuous habitation for the entirety of seven centuries. That is 24 generations; plus grand-children Rebecca and Sam who were down for the weekend.

Ostrich country, coming to the wire, at Scoles Farm.

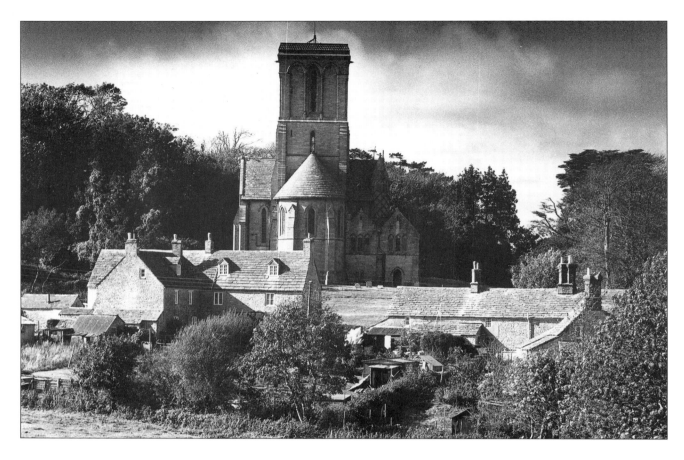

KINGSTON

St James's Church and East Street – 1975 (Colin Graham)

Architecturally rather than historically, the hamlet of Kingston has the finest church in the Isle of Purbeck, built to almost cathedral-like proportions by George Edmund Street between 1874 and 1880. It seen from the east, looking westwards from Kingston Hill, dwarfing terraces of stone-roofed cottages down in South Street. The southern hamlet in Corfe Castle parish, Kingston was rebuilt in its present form by the philanthropist William Morton Pitt. He built a cordage and sail-cloth works, provided model housing for the 200 workers, and opened the New Inn in 1787. Pitt's efforts fell apart when the Battle of Trafalgar took the bottom out of the naval market. The New Inn, became the Eldon Arms on the arrival of John Scott, 1st Earl of Eldon, and the Scott Arms after the Eldon title moved sideways from Encombe House.

Victorian Gothic, eastwards to the altar, in St James's Church at Kingston.

Lord Chancellor Eldon rebuilt the hamlet's historic church in 1833. A later John Scott, 3rd Earl of Eldon, decided to build an entirely new and imposing second St James's Church on the top of the rise beside South Street. He commissioned George Street to use Purbeck stone and marble in a convincing copy of thirteenth-century Gothic style which he called his 'jolliest' job. A year after it was finished, Street died, and his son described the Kingston work as 'one of the most complete things my father ever did'. Street's diary entries shows he also approved: 'I hope the interior will be beautiful. It ought to be for they have already spent a large sum of money on it. It will be difficult to find, even among old buildings, anything as thoroughly elaborated, I believe. It is a real pleasure to work for such a man as Lord Eldon.' Church architectural historian Fred Pitfield, in *Purbeck Parish Churches*, commends its authentic thirteenth-century details and the lavish use of Purbeck marble for the shafting of the arcade piers. Most of the stone came from the old quarries at Blashenwell.

KINGSTON

St James's Church and Kingston hamlet – 1997 (Rodney Legg)

The wider view from Kingston Hill takes in the 1856-built National School (right) though the Scott Arms for which it is known remains hidden in the trees.

Alfred Dawson's drawing of the newly completed church in 1882.

LANGTON MATRAVERS

Durnford School at Dancing Ledge – 1898

Thomas Pellatt established Durnford School in a rambling country house at the centre of the High Street in Langton Matravers. It had been Durnford House, the home of the Serrell family, from 1725 till the 1890s. Captain Serrell Rogers was the last to live there. Thomas and Ellinor Pellatt's daughter, Hester Wolferstan Pellatt who was born there in 1899, became known as the novelist and Tudor biographer Hester Chapman. She died in 1976. This preparatory, or boys' boarding school as it used to be known, catered for the seven to fourteen age group and concentrated on swimming, games and the rifle-range with the Dartmouth entrance examination in mind. The hardening process for Royal Navy entry requirements began with a compulsory walk, whatever the weather,

The swimming pool cut in the ledge for Durnford schoolboys.

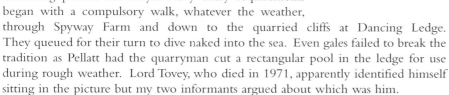

through Spyway Farm and down to the quarried cliffs at Dancing Ledge. They queued for their turn to dive naked into the sea. Even gales failed to break the tradition as Pellatt had the quarryman cut a rectangular pool in the ledge for use during rough weather. Lord Tovey, who died in 1971, apparently identified himself sitting in the picture but my two informants argued about which was him.

The last headmaster was C. L. Lee-Elliott. War closed Durnford School which was requisitioned in 1940 by the Telecommunications Research Establishment, based at Worth Matravers, and used with Langton House in the development of airborne and aerial ground-mapping radar apparatus which was deployed to devastating effect by the Royal Air Force through the second half of the conflict. By 1950 the Durnford buildings were empty and most were demolished by a new headmaster, Mr Haggard, in the process of establishing Malthouse School as its successor. Durnford preparatory pupil John Cronyn Tovey, born in 1885, returned to the village as Admiral of the Fleet, 1st Baron Tovey of Langton Matravers. He had a distinguished career through and between both wars which was crowned by lasting 'Sink the Bismarck' fame. On 14 May 1950 he unveiled a stained-glass window in the parish church in memory of his pals from Durnford who fell in the world wars, including some of the boys in our picture. The sermon was by the Bishop of Ludlow – another old boy – and the Admiral proudly pointed to Drake's Drum among the glazed saints.

LANGTON MATRAVERS

Dancing Ledge – 1989 (Rodney Legg)

A wider view to the east. In 1993 the National Trust acquired Spyway Farm with 190 acres of limestone downland including all the slopes around Dancing Ledge. This provided the title for the autobiography of avant-garde film producer Derek Jarman. He made risqué movies here, featuring friends and lovers, who were invariably without their clothes. It must be something about the place. Its last tripod-shaped derrick had a busy after-life following removal in 1930, being used by Walter and Treleven Haysom, in St Aldhelm's Quarry on St Alban's Head.

Ambushing a climber as he comes up over the edge.

Swanage & the Isle of Wight from
Langton Matravers. Aug. 28. 1882.

LANGTON MATRAVERS

High Street, in a Victorian sketch – 1882 (Sir James Peile)

Top end of the High Street, eastwards to the Isle of Wight, with seventeenth-century No 120 (left) and next-door No 114, which has varying roof levels and an inscription for 'S. C. 1799'. Behind are the Top House and Old Parliament House with Ballard Down across the fields (far left). On the other side of the street is Arundel Terrace (right) which comprises eight dwellings. Down the road, James Smith was at Garfield House, Captain Serrell Rogers at Durnford House, Miss Brodie in Elm House, Rev. Lester Lester at the Rectory, and Henry Stilwell in Leeson House.

Court Pound Cottage, across the road from Acton Field.

This was the upper part of a linear village, based around a single street which was an ancient ridgeway dating back to prehistoric Roman times. It was the main road for Sir James Peile's approach, en route to Swanage, while on vacation from the colonial service in Bombay. This was the first turnpiked road between Swanage and Corfe Castle – via Kingston – before completion of a direct valley-route through Harman's Cross. Mainly because of the stone trade, Langton's population was high for a Purbeck parish, being 892 in 1881.

LANGTON MATRAVERS

High Street – 2002 (Rodney Legg)

The western end of Langton Matravers is almost unchanged, with all its old buildings, plus the modern frying-pan shaped estate of Capston Field (far right). Despite the old spelling the name derives from the capstan or winch of a mule-hauled smack which pulled the chains to lift stone from one of the many slides or shafts which pepper these pastures. Across the field to the left, with a public path sign pointing towards it from the cottage, is Norman's Quarry. Here a perfect working has been preserved by the National Trust, which inherited the land with the Bankes Estate in 1982, as Ernie Norman last worked it in 1939. A grille prevents humans coming to grief underground, but lets the bats through, and a restored capstan and smack have been re-set between the original capstons. There are a couple of lengths of rail along which the stone was raised and removed to work-benches. Castle View used to be known as Mount Misery. Court Pound Cottage takes its name from an adjoining stone-walled enclosure where donkeys were impounded when they strayed from the quarries.

Crabstones, capstan and smack at Norman's Quarry.

Acton Field (right) is a camping site on Trust land. The National Trust also owns operational quarries, all now worked from above ground, at Acton and Worth Matravers. Victorian and Edwardian masons and merchants included James Albert Brown, Ambrose Bower and Thomas Albert Bower. Other family names attach to nearby mines and their sites – including Brown, Imany, Harris, Phippard, Short and Whistler – but these too can be repetitive. The Bowers were ubiquitous into the twentieth century. Blacksmith John made their tools, Job was the last shopkeeper in Acton, and Ernest was sub-postmaster in Langton Matravers.

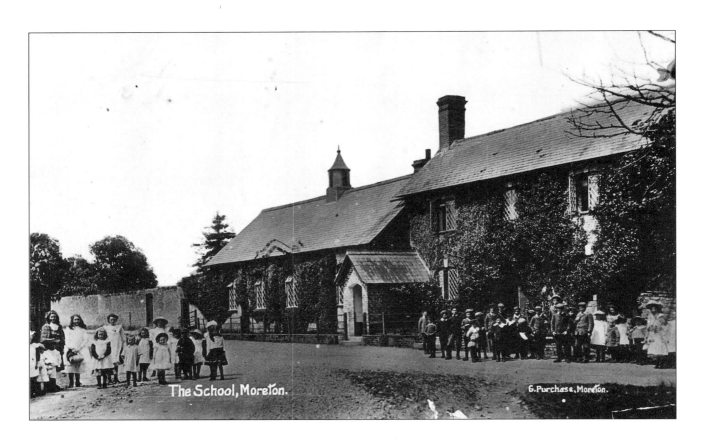

The School, Moreton.

G. Purchase, Moreton.

MORETON
Moreton School – 1910

Moreton, with its Frampton Arms public house a mile beside the railway line, remains an archetypal estate. There are still Framptons in Moreton House, built by James Frampton in 1744, though his prim Gothic-style church of 1777 is now a replica, having sustained a direct hit from a Luftwaffe bomb, and been rebuilt with the finest collection in the land of etched-glass windows by Sir Laurence Whistler. The Anglican National School, with adjoining school-house, was built in 1860 to cater for 120 children. At the turn of the century it became a public Elementary School, being taken over by Dorset County Council, under the Education Act of 1901. The view in the picture is looking north-westwards with the two groups of children separated by the road. Miss Louisa Talbot, the mistress, was followed by Miss Mary Collins. By 1885, in the time of schoolmistress Miss Hannah Uphill, attendance had dropped to 80.

Loco parentis seems to have shrunk into the background during this photo-call – perhaps taking the picture – but I am told the master was Alfred Connop. Miss Page was his assistant. Family names in the school register included Allen, Bale, Bowery, Brinson, Carpenter, Hansford, Hawkins, Hodder, Holden, Keats, Legg, Lovely, Pitman, Shrimpton, Trenet, Vincent and Wills. Miss Amy Grace Gillett, from across the meadows at Hurst, was the mistress during the Great War.

South front of the Old School House.

MORETON
Moreton Tea Rooms and Restaurant – 2002

The old schoolroom received a new lease of life in 2001 with the schoolroom being decorated with pictures of past pupils. Winston Churchill and Colonel Thomas Edward Lawrence also figure on the wall as a reminder that Moreton and this road junction topped the national news on Tuesday 21 May 1935. Churchill led the procession of mourners for Lawrence of Arabia, from his funeral in St Nicholas's Church, around the corner to the cemetery. Three special coaches had been added to the train from Waterloo but Major-General Archibald Wavell, veteran of the Palestine Campaign, upstaged other dignitaries by descending into the parkland in an experimental Autogiro.

The Old School House became the home of Margaret Selby. A bookcase survives in the schoolroom, provided for 'Coker's Library' which was a local charity established under the will of Rev. Roger Coker, the rector during the Napoleonic Wars.

Moreton Tea Rooms and Restaurant, in the old schoolroom, from the south-west.

Moreton.

MORETON

The Street, in a water-colour – 1904 (Walter Tyndale)

Eastwards along a long range of four thatched cottages, number 4 to 9, to a single small cottage and the thatched house adjoining the Post Office. The terrace of cottages spans the seventeenth to the nineteenth centuries with the architectural flourishes in the distance, with symmetrical frontages and casement windows, dating from the eighteenth century. Miss Matilda Kezia Looker was the grocer and postmistress at the Stores in the 1890s. By the time of the Great War the sub-postmaster was George Purchase. Letters arrived from Dorchester at 6.15 am and 12.50 pm each day. Outgoing mail was collected at noon and 6.45 pm. The latter time also applied for the single collection on Sundays.

The range of cottages in The Street from further out in the road.

MORETON

The Street – 2002 (Rodney Legg)

The Street at Moreton is one of those rare time-warps that has survived with hardly any expansion or in-filling. The loss has been of a small eighteenth-century dwelling which stood beyond the range of four cottages. It had a living room with an open fireplace and bread-oven, partitioned from a scullery, with the narrow bedroom stairs tucked away in one corner. This thatched cottage has been replaced by a modern house though the look of the street has been saved by the retention of thatch. Opposite is Wheelbarrow Cottage.

The same range of cottages from the other direction, looking north-westwards.

Moreton's wider landscape was dominated for years, on Fir Hill towards the railway line, by an obelisk. This is now almost lost in the trees. It originally stood in the 100-acre park surrounding Moreton House, having been erected in 1785 by Captain John Houlton, in memory of his friend James Frampton. The stone urn on the top is said to weigh four tons. James Frampton had often thought of building on top of Fir Hill. It 'would have good effect' he wrote in the estate diary. Marble tablets from the plinth of the obelisk have been removed and brought back to the village, being re-set in the lych-gate to the cemetery, where it causes some puzzlement to visitors searching for the grave of T. E. Lawrence.

OWER

Ower Quay – 1971 (Rodney Legg)

The most peaceful and poignant place in the Isle of Purbeck is the point from which immense quantities of Purbeck marble were exported during the Middle Ages. This is the view north-westwards to Fitzworth (left) and the South Deep (right) through Poole Harbour. Purbeck marble is a hard fossiliferous freshwater limestone rather than a true marble. Its virtue is that it takes a fine polish, being widely used in Roman times, and came back into vogue for making effigies. These include that of King John in Worcester Cathedral, carved in about 1240, which is the earliest royal effigy in England. When Henry III enlarged Westminster Abbey the surveyors purchased 'the King's marble in Purbeck for the King's work in Westminster'. Salisbury Cathedral consumed masses of Purbeck as it arose between 1220 to 1258 to reach the finest peak of Early English style. Shafts of Purbeck marble grace many of the other greatest churches in the land, including the cathedrals of Chichester, Ely, Exeter, Wells, Winchester and Worcester, and the magnificent Temple Church in London. Many abbeys and several bishop's palaces were also built with Purbeck marble for their finery but most were destroyed after the Reformation.

The path to the water, beside the cottage, at Ower Quay.

Effigies and ecclesiastical masonry were often carved in Corfe Castle. The accounts of the Sheriff of Dorset for 1254 record the payment to masons there of 100 shillings: 'For carving a certain effigy of a Queen in marble stone, carrying it to Tarrant Crawford, and placing it there over the tomb of the Queen of Scotland.' That one went by road rather than sea but most were pulled on sledges across the heath to Ower, such as two tombs of marble for the Earl of Arundel and his lady, plus 'one great stone' for the Bishop of Winchester which were put aboard the 48-ton vessel *Margarete*, from Wareham, in 1374. She was seized for use in an expedition against the French but was released after the intervention of her influential paymasters. Peppercorn Lane, eastwards from Bushey, takes its name from the 1695 agreement by the Company of Marblers and Stonecutters of Purbeck to pay John Collins of Ower a pound of pepper each Shrove Tuesday. A football was kicked along the track in an annual ceremony to retain the right-of-way. From 1710 the operational end of the stone trade has been based between Worth Matravers and Swanage.

OWER

Ower Quay – 2000 (Rodney Legg)

Little now remains to show the former importance of Ower Quay. The stumps of the old jetty are rotting in the mud and even nearby stones, dumped as a shore protection measure, are lumps of alien geology from Devon and the Mendip Hills. Offshore, another line of 16 posts are the timbers of an old ship that was a floating café, early in the twentieth century. The nearby cottage has one of the best settings in Purbeck.

Reflections of the past in tranquil waters at Ower Quay.

REMPSTONE
Stone Circle – 1964 (Rodney Legg)

The only surviving Bronze Age stone circle in the Isle of Purbeck, looking south-eastwards to King's Wood, on the northern slope of Nine Barrow Down. The 'probable' dating by the Royal Commission on Historical Monuments is to about 2500 BC in the early Bronze Age. These gritty boulders from the underlying Bagshot Beds were not noted in print until 1908, in the *Proceedings of the Dorset Natural History and Archaeological Field Club*, in which the Rev. C. V. Goddard is quoted from a letter of 1900, saying 'my wife took me into a wood just beyond Rempstone, on the road to Studland, and we at once found ourselves in what I have no doubt is the remaining segment of a stone circle'. Nelson Richardson read Goddard's notes to a meeting at Studland: 'They are all chocolate-coloured iron gritstone, and flattish in section. Nine are set round in just about (the northern) half of the circle or a little more, and measure 24 paces from the south-east one to the tall north-east one'.

The north-western stones, towards a passing car on the Studland road.

This is the one in my picture, bearing the Government's broad-arrow as a bench-mark at 3 feet above the ground, for the point the Ordnance Survey puts at 278 feet above sea level. Two more can be seen behind, one standing and the other at an angle, in a temporary view after the wood had been felled. The circle is 80 feet in diameter and crossed by ditches and a bank, in the middle distance, beyond which are the boggy depressions of eighteenth-century claypits. These are shown on a map of 1772 and caused the removal of all but three of the southern stones. Eight survive in their original positions on the northern half. There are some gaps and the original complement must have been about 25 stones. Some of the displaced stones lie elsewhere in the wood. Half a mile to the west, after ploughing in 1957, Langton Matravers headmaster and archaeologist J. Bernard Calkin discovered a double alignment of smaller stones. 'They may have formed a processional way', he told me.

REMPSTONE
Stone Circle – 2002 (Rodney Legg)

The view has scrubbed-up again and it is now impossible to see more than two or three of the stones at a time. However, it now receives a regular attendance from admirers, with candles, coins and other votive offerings to show that it is in regular use as a pagan shrine.

There was another Purbeck stone circle. The antiquary Charles Warne recorded in 1872 that he was told by John Fitzgerald Pennie that one stood 'within living memory between East Lulworth and Povington, but not a vestige

Displaced stones lying beside old claypits in the copse at Rempstone.

of it remains'. The stones were taken away by farmer Bower and used for gateposts and a bridge. While compiling *Purbeck Island* in 1972 I came across the remarkable coincidence of another Rempstone placename – Rempstone Gate – where the heathland road into the Lulworth Ranges crosses the Tyneham parish boundary.

STUDLAND

Cross Tree and Cart-Shed – 1895

The junction beside Manor Farm and Studland Dairy, looking eastwards from Church Road, to the village Cart-Shed (left) and the Cross Tree with the heathstone base of a Saxon cross beside it on the mound (right). The notice reads: 'Any persons stealing ferns, sand, earth or peat will be prosecuted without further notice. By Order.'

The base of the Saxon cross, the only one to survive in the Isle of Purbeck, comprises a single block of gritty local ironstone, 4 feet in diameter and 2 feet high, with a socket hole. Manor Farm, the south-eastern extremity of the lands of Walter Bankes of Kingston Lacy House, was tenanted by Thomas Chinchen Horlock.

The Cart-Shed houses a 1942-built Fordson tractor.

STUDLAND

Cross and Cart-Shed – 2002 (Rodney Legg)

Remarkably, despite the loss of the tree and barns in the background when Studland Dairy was destroyed by fire on 8 August 1908, the Cart-Shed survives and the Cross has been re-erected. Its ancient base from the first Christian millennium saw resurrection just in time for the third, after much cajoling of villagers by rector and Canon Douglas O'Hanlon who arrived in 1972. He chipped away at 'resistance and reluctance' and funds were raised for a new shaft to be 'quarried and carved' by sculptor Treleven Haysom, son of Walter Haysom, at St Aldhelm's Quarry on St Alban's Head. The east-facing side is a tour-de-force in symbols of the world, natural and man-made – arising from two ears of wheat into the double-helix of DNA – embracing a violin, bomb, Concorde, butterfly and Christ. Treleven Haysom chose the subjects. This must be the first DNA sample in bas-relief on a consecrated stone. The outer strands entwine into a cross at the top. Oddly, the 12-feet high Cross was consecrated, but not its carvings, as Canon O'Hanlon explained to me at the time. It was still a blank stone canvas when Dr George Reindorp, Bishop of Salisbury, arrived on 24 July 1975 to carry out the ceremony, and then it had to be taken back to the quarry for completion. Hell is on the dark side, facing north, and the south side spells out a message in Celtic-style Dark Age runes: 'I created this world and I sustain this world.'

Concorde, bomb and violin on Treleven Haysom's cross.

The Cart-Shed, having survived against all the odds, was the smallest of the buildings on the estate inventory that passed to the National Trust after the death of Ralph Bankes in 1981. It now houses a 1942-built Fordson tractor, a robust machine with interchangeable iron wheels to increase its versatility, which is still in working order. It is on loan from Manor Farm Museum on the other side of the road.

STUDLAND

St Nicholas's Church – 1880

Ivy-clad neglect masked a bigger problem within. The central tower arches of one of only a handful or two of complete Norman churches in England were bulging with 'immense cracks' and threatening 'utter collapse'. Its squat and venerable appearance, looking north-eastwards in this photograph, had been accentuated by this inherent weakness, dating from about 1150. The builders began adding another six feet of masonry to top off the tower but stopped when the increasing weight caused cracks above the arches. Seven centuries later, Weymouth architect George Crickmay commissioned Swanage builder William Masters Hardy to save the day, with bracing and underpinning. This accomplished, in 1881, Hardy was confident that the tower could be finished off to its intended height. That work, however, was never done. He did, however, strip the ivy and rebuild the porch.

In the churchyard the gravestone in the front of the porch is that of Sergeant William Lawrence. He ran away from the village as an apprentice and took the King's shilling with the 40th Regiment of Foot. Having gone through the South American campaigns and the Peninsular War – suffering serious wounds in storming Badajoz on 6 April 1812 – he fought at Waterloo on 18 June 1815. Back home, despite disabilities, he walked from Bristol to Glasgow on failing to find a ship, and was seconded to the Coastguard service in Ireland before retiring in 1820. Taking on the New Inn in Studland he renamed it the Duke of Wellington in honour of his old commander. It is now the Bankes Arms.

Biographical gravestone of Waterloo veteran Sergeant William Lawrence.

STUDLAND

St Nicholas's Church – 2002 (Rodney Legg)

The view remains the same though you have to shift sideways to avoid blocking it with foliage. The nave roof was reconstructed in 1931. Victorian builder William Masters Hardy had discovered Roman burials and more have been found. In 1951, excavation of a stone cist in the churchyard by J. Bernard Calkin revealed the skeleton of a woman with a severed head, detached after death. Her skeleton is exhibited in Red House Museum at Christchurch.

Research into the church, by the Royal Commission on Historical Monuments in 1970, revealed that the Norman ornamentation has been inserted into Saxon walls: 'The church was probably built shortly before the Conquest, with chancel, central tower and nave.' This original floor-plan survives as does the inner core of both the chancel and tower walls. It may be of some significance in terms of dating that the chancel is aligned towards east-south-east and is therefore slightly out of line with the west-east walls of the nave and tower. Southwards, beside the gate into the churchyard from Church Road, stone-roofed Saint Nicholas Hall was built in 1952.

St Nicholas Hall, shaded by trees, beside the churchyard entrance.

STUDLAND
Watery Lane – 1900

The cottages in Watery Lane, looking south-eastwards into the track leading to Harry Warren House and chalk cliffs south of Studland Bay, to Old Harry Rocks. Dating from the eighteenth century, they are semi-detached single-storey homes with attic rooms tucked under the thatch, and fire-places in the east and west gable ends. That is about the limit of visual inspection and their entry in the report of the Royal Commission on Historical Monuments provides just two words in the style of a football score: 'Cottages, two.'

The cottages at Watery Lane in the late Victorian times.

While compiling *The Book of Studland* I came across some old notes in which Mrs May Worley Morton recalled having her portrait painted here, as a child, with the wife of Scottish artist Edwin Alexander. She also recalled Mr and Mrs Alexander's 'coloured servant peeling potatoes and counting them into a saucepan'. Antarctic explorer Captain Robert Falcon Scott stayed with the Alexanders on the cliff at Studland in 1909, shortly before setting off on his last great adventure in the *Terra Nova*. That year a Captain Scott from Studland was convicted of driving a motor car at 'excessive speed' in Swanage ('more than 19 miles per hour') and failed to produce his licence. He was fined £2 with 19 shillings costs.

STUDLAND
Watery Lane – 2002 (Rodney Legg)

This is another of our views that survives almost unchanged from the architectural point of view but has almost completely scrubbed-up. A glimpse from the overgrown hedge-bank, obstructed by a telegraph pole, is the best that can be offered. In the foreground there are flowers of Himalayan balsam, a Victorian introduction that has made itself at home in the countryside, characterised by lush foliage, pink flowers and seed pods that explode as they are touched.

Nos. 2 and 3 Watery Lane, looking southwards, from the wall of the public toilets.

On the other hand, looking south at the full view of the frontage, their appearance is much the same. What you do not see from comparative photographs is that such a view, these days, will have been taken from public toilets that do brisk business through the summer. Queues are likely as ramblers and school parties come down the path from Old Harry Rocks. That has been the down-side, literally, for the occupants of this little piece of paradise, who in recent years have been William Millard followed by Angela Waterman in number 2 and Joseph and Patricia Parish in number 3.

SWANAGE

Clock Tower and Lifeboat Station – 1893

12-004 is the Swanage Lifeboat.

From the Battery behind the Coastguard Cottages on Peveril Point, westwards to the Clock Tower (left), and the Lifeboat Station (right). The mortar and cannon belonged to No 7 Battery of the 2nd Volunteer Brigade, Southern Division, of the Royal Artillery. James Houghton was their drill instructor. The Wellington Clock Tower was erected beside the Southwark end of London Bridge in 1854 – commemorating the Iron Duke, victor of Waterloo and former Prime Minister who died in 1852 – but suffered three failings. Firstly its state of the art clock, made for the Great Exhibition in 1851, failed to cope with vibration from the passing traffic. Secondly the structure was condemned by the Metropolitan Police as 'an unwarrantable obstruction'. Thirdly and finally railway lines blocked its main view, in 1863, and it was demolished in 1866. This coincided with contractor Thomas Docwra buying The Grove, beside Peveril Downs, and Mowlem and Company presented him with the tower. Docwra had the monument shipped to Swanage and rebuilt beside the foreshore in the north-east corner of his walled grounds. Two villas, Peveril Tower (later named Rockleigh) and Sunnydown were built near it in the early 1890s, by next owner Edwin Williams.

The Lifeboat Station was constructed for the *Charlotte Mary* in 1875. Her coxswain was William Masters who provided lodgings at West End Cottage for author Thomas Hardy and appears in *The Hand of Ethelberta* as Captain Flower. His wife features in the poem 'The Lodging House Fuchsias'. In 1890 the second Swanage Lifeboat was *William Erle*, donated by Lady Erle in memory of her husband, Chief Justice Sir William Erle, which proved unstable and was replaced by a second vessel of the same name in 1893. The first lifeboat to arrive in Swanage, incidentally, was the *Mary Heape* on 21 November 1866. Hauled by road from Wareham Station, she was sponsored by Miss E. M. Scott and launched by her at a reception hosted by the 2nd Earl of Eldon, but then sailed along the coast to be based in the newly established Kimmeridge Lifeboat Station.

SWANAGE

Clock Tower and Lifeboat Station – 2001 (Rodney Legg)

Until 1904 the Clock Tower had an attractive spire but this was replaced by a cupola, after Christian fundamentalist protests that spires should only be seen on churches. The Lifeboat Station was extended in 1991, with a new slipway, for the Mersey-class *Robert Charles Brown*, which was the first Swanage Lifeboat to be named for a local lifeboatman rather than a benefactor.

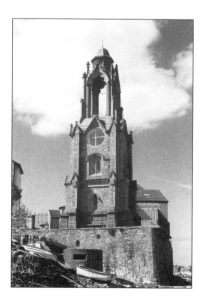

The Duke of Wellington's memorial Clock Tower, with an anti-invasion pillbox from 1940, tucked into the foundations.

SWANAGE

Court Road – 1892 (Walter Pouncy)

Court Road, or Old Gilbert Road, with Carrants Court (left) looking north-eastwards down Court Hill. Opposite there was a farmyard and stone-lined rectangle of water with adjoining duck-pond that was known as the Lake. Deriving from the Old English word 'lacu' it is a common name for a water-course in Purbeck. The picture has been taken from the Albert Memorial erected to 'Albert the Good' – Queen Victoria's consort – who visited Swanage in 1849 and died in 1861. His monument was erected the following year by Swanage mason, contractor and benefactor John Mowlem who was born in a cottage at Carrants Court in 1788. The memorial was given fulsome praise in J. G. Harrod's *Directory of Dorsetshire* for 1865: 'Small as Swanage is at present, it has displayed, in proportion to its limits, a highly loyal patriotic feeling. In doing justice to the memory of Albert the Good, the inhabitants were among the foremost. A very chaste and well-proportioned obelisk, with an appropriate inscription, was erected by the north side of the road above the Cemetery, at a point where it is seen for a considerable distance in either direction of the highway, and it at once forms a beautiful foreground object to the view of the valley, and a very interesting one in all the views from it.'

Ivydene, below Carrants Court, is No. 6 Court Road.

SWANAGE

Court Road – 2001 (Rodney Legg)

The setting and the architecture have not fared too well. Only one stone-roofed house remains, eighteenth-century Ivydene (left side, centre), among modern houses. This was the Grant family's Court Hill farmhouse. Opposite, further down the hill, are Court Hill Wines and the Kingdom Hall of Jehovah's Witnesses. The Homestead is on the corner with King's Road and the shed is the King's Road Depot of Purbeck District Council. A triangular slope in the foreground, in the angle between Court Road and the High Street, has been landscaped with shrubs.

What has disappeared, with not a trace left behind, is John Mowlem's memorial to 'Albert the Good' which was demolished after a dispute with developers in 1971. Two decades later, after an anonymous tip-off from a Swanage resident, I rediscovered it 4 miles away to the south-west in St Aldhelm's Quarry on St Alban's Head. It was stacked in sections. I photographed the 'Albert' and 'Good' inscriptions in capital letters and Roman numerals with Prince Albert's dates. No one responded to my suggestion that it should be rebuilt for the next major royal occasion. That should now be Queen Elizabeth's diamond jubilee in 2012, which may well be followed in 2015 by the all-time achievement, overtaking that of Queen Victoria, of the longest reign on record. The logical link would be a unique monument to both of their consorts.

Displaced parts of 'Albert' (centre) the 'Good' (upside down, below) stacked in St Aldhelm's Quarry.

33   SWANAGE. — *High Street.* — LL.

SWANAGE

High Street and Town Hall – 1905

The central part of the High Street, looking eastwards from Virginia Cottage and Fred Cox's boot and shoe shop (left). In front of York House are watchmaker Thomas S. Hayward's Curiosity Shop and the dilapidated premises of Francis Hendon, greengrocer and florist (right). The distinguished building (centre left) is the Town Hall which carries inscriptions with two dates and locations. 'Cheapside 1670' became 'Swanage 1882'. The baroque frontage, strikingly tall with two lofty storeys as grandiose as any as London arose from the Great Fire of 1666, graced the Mercers' Hall. It has often been attributed to Sir Christopher Wren but the designer was in fact Edward Jerman and its builder was John Oliver.

Demolition took place in 1861 and Swanage-born contractor George Burt piled the stone in his Greenwich yard before the opportunity arose for shipping it to his home town. The Drong Cottages in the High Street ('drong' or 'drang' is Dorset dialect for an alleyway) were demolished in 1881 and Swanage was provided with its first purpose-built municipal building. Designs were by architect George Crickmay of Weymouth and at the opening ceremony in 1883 it was named King Alfred's Hall. Walking by on the other side, with straw hat and walking stick, is architect James Clifton who was in partnership with Edmund Robinson from Newton Manor. The first of the parade of shops in York Buildings behind – built in 1895 – was William Dixon's bakery.

The Mercers' Hall from London flying the flag in Swanage for Queen Elizabeth II's golden jubilee.

SWANAGE

High Street and Town Hall – 2002 (Rodney Legg)

Virginia Cottage and next door Wesley Cottage, where the preacher John Wesley stayed, were devastated by a German bomb in 1941. Successive occupiers of Hayward's Curiosity Shop and Hendon's greengrocers fell foul of what they called the 'Masonic Mafia' based across the road in the Town Hall. Petty complaints started over a 'turtle-shell advertisement' and went on with similar banalities until 1959 when York House was demolished for a new cinema. 'Television stopped that in the 1960s as cinemas became bingo halls,' I was told. 'It was then a much needed car-park until Burr Stone Mead was built on the site by the Shaftesbury Society housing association.'

Cupids and swags flank a female bust with babies above the central doorway.

The gable-end of Purbeck Valet dry cleaning is beside the alleyway to York Terrace and No. 81 High Street survives to the right, as does the wall of No. 87. Opposite at No. 66 are the 1989-built terrace of Wesley Gardens and a circular commemorative stone from Wesley's Cottage. Recovered from a garden in Fontmell Magna, it was unveiled by Bryan Hancock, the Mayor, in 1975. The inscription was up-dated: 'In a cottage on this site John Wesley stayed 12-13 October, 1774. The cottage was destroyed by enemy action 14 May 1941.'

SWANAGE

High Street westwards – 1885

The central section of the High Street, looking west from opposite Handfast Terrace, to the junction with Cowlease and Priests Road (left of centre). Here a typical Swanage cottage became Albert Frank Parker's grocery shop.

Stone was still being brought down from numerous quarries on the hillside above Cowlease which was the entrance to the Townsend workings. Swanage at this time was on the cusp of modernity with the parkland grounds to the right soon to become a building site. Its houses, Gordon Villas, would take their name from a hero of the British Empire, General Charles George Gordon, who as Governor of Sudan was the only Englishman in Khartoum after his two companions were murdered. Having repelled besieging forces for ten months, Gordon's martyrdom came when the Sudanese capital fell, on 26 January 1885. Relief was only days' marching distance away but that only added to this very British kind of triumphal failure.

Parker's Stores characterises old Swanage.

SWANAGE

High Street west to Parker's Stores – 2001 (Rodney Legg)

Opposite, on the south side of the central High Street, the two-storey and three-storey stone buildings have survived. The latter houses a hairdressing salon. Red-brick houses have appeared (left and centre), plus Durnford Place, and a stone-built terrace with bay-windows of Gordon Villas (opposite). Along the street, opposite the Priests Road and Cowlease junction, is the Union flag on its pole beside the Royal British Legion Club. Parker's Stores survives in business.

The Old Curiosity Shop and Hendon's green-grocery were demolished in 1959.

It rambles around a cramped corner with roads on either side. Low ceilings with exposed beams, and attic rooms tucked under roofs of stone slates at varying levels, typify early nineteenth-century Swanage. Quarries up to the left are now all a thing of the past and under a mix of houses, caravans and nature-reserve scrub. Eastwards along the High Street such scenes are now extinct. The Narrows and Wesley's Cottage were wiped off the map following wartime bombing. Opposite the Town Hall, the Old Curiosity Shop and Hendon's green-grocery followed, in 1959. Replaced by a housing project, promoted by the Shaftesbury Society, the spot now has the look of High Street anywhere. Only the Black Swan, rearing up from a raised pavement, sustains an intermittent continuity of character along the south side of the street between Purbeck House Hotel and Parker's Stores.

A Shaftesbury Society housing project replaced the Old Curiosity Shop.

SWANAGE

Mill Pond – 1892 (Walter Pouncy)

The Mill Pond, looking northwards from Church Hill, to elm trees beside Brewery Road and the distant line of Ballard Down. It looks like it has been here for ever, but was not created around the springs until 1754, and later enlarged. Gas-lighting came to Swanage in 1868. At the north end of the pond (centre, background) John Rawles had taken over as miller in 1884. Church Farm (right) was in the process of being divided and converted into what became seven cottage-style flats and tenements.

The parish church of St Mary the Virgin is beyond the frame (right). Rev. Thomas Alfred Gurney of St John's College, Cambridge, became the rector in 1887. He was succeeded by Rev. W. A. Wilson who died in 1905 and was briefly followed by his chosen heir – Rev. William Henry Parsons – who swapped parishes in 1908 with Rev. Henry Edwyn Eardley from Tunbridge Wells.

Southward view across the Mill Pond to Church Hill and the High Street.

SWANAGE

Mill Pond – 2002 (Rodney Legg)

The safety wall had already spoilt the view by the end of the nineteenth century. The terrace of cottages were rebuilt as Westwood, Millbrook and Blechynden in 1906 and 1907. John Rawles proved to be the last miller, with the Mill being sold by the Burt Estate in 1921, to builders Parsons and Hayter for £700. Machinery was scrapped during the Second World War though the wheel was re-set as a feature later in the century. An inscription has also been preserved for Southampton mill-wright Benjamin Barlow.

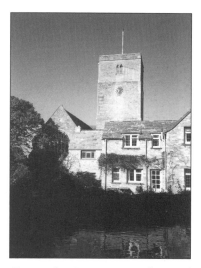

Eastward view into Mill Pond reflections, topped by the tower of St Mary's Church.

Cramped flats and tenements created out of former Church Farm (right) were condemned as slums in 1937 but spared from demolition provided improvements brought them into a condition 'suitable for human habitation'. Bureaucracy was delayed by war and austerity, with 'closing orders' being followed by 'demolition orders' and rebuilding eventually taking place in 1963, to designs by local architect Fred Walsh. He also rebuilt Coniston Close which overlooks the Mill Pond from the south, behind the photographer, on the slope towards the High Street. Dutch elm disease defoliated the view early in the 1970s. Brewery Road became King's Road East within a year or two of the earlier photograph. In the other direction, in the triangle formed by the junction of Church Hill with the High Street a cross was raised in 1909, in memory of amateur stone-carver Sir Reginald Palgrave who was Clerk of the House of Commons from 1886 to 1900. Facing it, Wyvern Cottage has stones for 'W. C. 1793' and the more auspicious year 1940, to mark repairs after German bombing.

SWANAGE
Mowlem's Column – 1905

Drinking fountain (foreground) and John Mowlem's Column, with a cluster of four cannon balls on top, looking north-westwards across the remains of Eastbrook Farm after the completion of the Promenade. The Swanage-born contractor made his fortune paving and rebuilding London with Purbeck stone and even cheaper and more accessible 'good blue granite' from Guernsey. He boasted that one freehold quarry had cost him £50 for a total of half a million tons of stone. Ten thousand tons to the pound worked out at more than ten tons for a farthing. His brig the *John Mowlem* carried out a triangular trade between London, Swanage and the Channel Islands with cargoes of coal and discarded pieces of capital architecture being among the ballast brought to Dorset.

The Mowlem and Mowlem's Column in a seaward view.

Returning to Swanage in 1845, Mowlem bought No. 2 Victoria Terrace on the seaside and built Herston House as his country mansion. Having had a leading role in providing the first timber pier in 1859, he decided to give the town a little history, by commemorating a victory over the Vikings in 877. The Anglo Saxon Chronicle, however, makes it clear that the disaster for the Danes in Swanage Bay was by shipwreck in a gale. Mowlem disregarded the facts and erected his commemorative column in 1862, further muddling the history by topping it with Russian shells, from ships returning to Portsmouth from Crimean War actions in the Black Sea and Baltic. Sir Frederick Treves ridiculed it: 'Cannon balls suggest battle, but there has been no battle at Swanage. King Alfred, however, is supposed to have defeated the Danes in Swanage Bay in the year of our Lord 877. Naturally enough, the contractor erected a pillar on the Marine Parade to commemorate this proud if dim event, and placed the cannon balls on top of it. To some these missiles may appear inappropriate, as gunpowder was not invented until more than 400 years after the assumed engagement.'

SWANAGE
Mowlem's Column (Rodney Legg)

The view now is to the parade of shops with Forte's ice-cream parlour and a bouncy castle on the triangular grassy rise between Shore Road, Station Place and Mermaid Place. Mowlem's Column had its battle for survival when Swanage Urban District Council met in October 1965. Councillor A. E. R. Gray led the artillery. 'It's historically inaccurate,' he said, 'and the balls on top look like a pawnbroker's sign. The day of monuments had passed. This one should be demolished and sunk to the bottom of the bay.' Members divided on the issue but voted to spend £200 on moving the monument a few feet rather than £75 for demolition.

John Mowlem's bust from the original Mowlem Institute.

The seafront building (left), built in 1914, was Thomas Powell's photographic studio from 1916. Originally decked-out with massive letters for 'Kodaks' it was managed by his son William Powell. Between them they took many of our pictures.

The Sands, West Bay, Swanage. W8717.

SWANAGE

New Swanage – 1904

The sands of New Swanage, separated from the town by farms and fields, looking northwards to Highcliffe Road and Ulwell Road (far left). Sea Bank Lodge, the home of beach trader Frank Parsons, is on the first level of the cliff (left). Higher up, the Monte Rosa is at the seaward end of Highcliffe Road and the Grand Hotel can just be glimpsed (centre right) towards the former Pondfield Cove below Ballard Down. It was built in 1898.

Coachman and bathing tent proprietor Thomas Shiner brought 'Mixed Bathing' to Swanage in 1879. Wife Elizabeth continued the business into the new century and Tom Shiner was still a 'bathing tent proprietor' in 1935. He sold 'Swanage rock' from a kiosk on the esplanade in Shore Road. Further south along the beach, in Edwardian times, John Davis White's bathing machine catered as a 'Bathing Saloon for Gentlemen' and Lillington's advertised 'Ladies Only'. Individual 'Hygienic Bathing Tents' were pushed to the water on wheels.

Beach-hut user and one toddler (right) not quite making a summer.

SWANAGE

New Swanage – 2001 (Rodney Legg)

The Grand Hotel remains one of the town's main hotels but the Monte Rosa has been rebuilt and expanded into a block of flats. More changes have happened in the foreground as the coast road from old Swanage, Beach Road, became Shore Road. Firstly, in May 1906, Frank Parsons built a timber shack with a veranda which he called Beach Refreshment Room. There was a stone-built terrace for tables and perambulators and a short staircase, of eight steps, led down on the beach where Parsons hired deck-chairs and boats. A few yards to the north, employees in a second kiosk organised double lines of bathing tents, for changing one's clothes into beach-

Opening-up time at Ocean Bay Watersports.

ware. By 1908 business was so brisk that Parsons replaced his shed with a battle-mented and colonnaded structure (left foreground), designed by Bournemouth architect Thomas Grimes, and traded as Beach Restaurant and Stores. This also became the Post Office for New Swanage and offered self-catering accommodation in adjoining rooms. Other members of the Parsons family established holiday apartments across the town – Frederick at Glenthorn in Ulwell Road; Harold at The Whim in Queen's Road; John at Sea Side Villa, Ulwell Road; and Miss L. M. Parsons at The Bungalow in Burlington Road. John Davis White, the last old-style bathing machine operator, died in 1927.

The successor to Beach Restaurant and Stores, Ocean Bay Watersports, is seen with an empty beach and appears out of season in June thanks to a combination adverse circumstances. The millennium opened with closure of the countryside, due to a foot-and-mouth epidemic, and more of the cool, dull weather that has characterised recent summers.

SWANAGE
Oldfeld – 1916 (Thomas Powell)

The pastures between the old town and New Swanage (near left) from Oldfeld House, looking south-eastwards over Walrond Road and de Moulham Villas to central Swanage and Peveril Point (far left). This picture has come from Mark and Rachel Helfer at Knitson Old Farmhouse.

Purbeck Heights School dominating the view southwards across Walrond Road.

SWANAGE
Purbeck Heights School – 2002 (Rodney Legg)

My apologies for the vegetation, but this was the best I could do, even after having climbed on a wall. 'Typical male,' a teacher sighed, because of the bad example that was being set.

The hilltop viewpoint on the west side of Northbrook Road, north of Walrond Road and opposite Beach Gardens, is dominated by the buildings of the former Forres School. This was established in Northwood, Middlesex, in 1908 by Arthur Joseph Chadwick. Then Chadwick died, in 1912, and the school was taken over by Rohan McKenzie Chadwick, his younger brother. Meanwhile, in Swanage, Brookfield House School was founded by Hugh Saunders in Victoria Avenue. The two schools merged as Forres in 1919 after Rohan Chadwick followed the new fashion for moving boarding schools to 'the healthier environs of the seaside'. The central section of the new school at Oldfeld, named for the family of early nineteenth-century rector Rev. Thomas Oldfeld Bartlett, was built in 1919. Forres School took its name to commemorate the Chadwick family's Elginshire roots. It was a boarding and day preparatory school, for boys and girls, between seven and thirteen-years-old. The west section was added in 1926. Fields to the north-east were laid out with the plots of Cauldron Avenue and Battlemead in 1933. Most of the houses were built in 1934. Beyond, Day's Park and sports fields take their name from greengrocer and dairyman Jimmy Day of Institute Road who also endowed the James Day Home. Post-war, the Forres School suffered Swanage's principal peacetime tragedy of the twentieth century when five of its boys were killed and two wounded, as they prodded a rusty canister in a rock pool at New Swanage on Friday 13 May 1955. It was one of 58 mines which had been missed during the post-war clearance of beach defences.

The view north-eastwards, to Ballard Down, is also compromised by leaves and roofs.

SWANAGE

Pier Approach – 1893 (William Powell)

The view is westwards to the Stone Quay. The access road in the foreground is to The Grove, the home of contractor Thomas Docwra, which was bought by Edwin Williams in the 1890s. Beyond, with the kiosk, is the entrance to the 1859-built timber Pier which was constructed by James Walton of London. Beyond are two public slipways and boat-hauls for fishermen and pleasure boat owners on a rocky foreshore accessible from the eastern extremity of the High Street. Next is the Stone Quay, projecting to the low-water mark and with a parapet on this side, making it usable only on east side. Inland from it, obscured by trees, is the Royal Victoria Hotel. Princess Victoria's visit was overnight on 7 August 1833.

Waverley arrival, in 2001, with stumps of the 1859-built pier in the foreground.

Eastwards, into the town as far as Institute Road, the 1863-built Mowlem Institute, and Eastbrook Farm, are high piles of cut building stone, paving and kerbing at the Stone Bankers. Before the opening of the 550-feet timber pier, in September 1861, stone used to be exported by high-wheeled carts wading into the bay, to ships standing offshore.

SWANAGE

Pier Approach – 2001 (Rodney Legg)

The foreground wall (left) disguises the subterranean world of the Sewage Works. The cars on the freshly laid tarmac (right) are at the back of the Boat Park behind Swanage Yacht Club. Cars behind the next wall are those of users of the second timber Pier, designed by R. St George Moore and built by Alfred Thorne of Westminster in 1895, to a length of 642 feet with an average width of 28 feet, expanding into a two-tier landing stage at the end. Its predecessor, last used for deliveries of coal, fell into disuse in the 1920s, becoming a skeleton of stumps by the 1970s.

Waverley departure, reversing out into Swanage Bay.

Its successor seemed to be going the same way, until a majority share in Swanage Pier Company was transferred from the receivers of Durrant Developments (Swanage Yacht Haven) Limited to Purbeck District Council, for a token £1 sum, in 1992. There was also a £125,000 cheque from the receivers to the local authority 'to release them from any obligations to maintain the Pier' under the Harbours Act of 1964. *Lord Elgin* had been the first paddle-steamer to arrive at the second Pier on May Day in 1896. The *Waverley* paddle-steamer celebrated its renaissance with a series of trips in September 2001 after £1.1 million had been spent on the rescue of the historic grade-II listed structure from lottery and other sources. Paul Croft of Purbeck District Council is Secretary of Swanage Pier Company. He says commercial income will always been swallowed by the cost of upkeep: 'Everything made on the Pier is ploughed back into its maintenance. At the moment there is not enough to put aside proper provision for further renovation. We have to face the fact that it is never going to be a profit-maker.'

SWANAGE
Stone Bankers and (Old) Pier – 1887

The Stone Bankers beside the Backwater and Brook, south-eastwards from the Mowlem Institute to Peveril Point and the 1859-built timber Pier. The earlier Stone Pier (right) is hosting a regatta to celebrate Queen Victoria's golden jubilee. A tramway led from the Bankers to the Pier. The Grove, the seaside home of London contractor Thomas Docwra, is hidden in the trees between Marine Villas and Peveril Down. Regency period Marine Villas (originally a single Marine Villa) were built by William Morton Pitt of Encombe House as his seaside summer house in 1825. It was purely for pleasure, with baths, coffee room and billiard room and hosted its first visit of royalty and gentry when the Duke of Gloucester led a party of yachtsmen from Lulworth Cove in 1828.

Stone Quay with a kiosk for Marsh's Pleasure Boats.

SWANAGE
The Mowlem and (New) Pier – 2001

What has come and gone from the view, with only a couple of classical columns left behind, was the transformation of Thomas Docwra's home at The Grove into the 400-feet frontage of the Hotel Grosvenor along the seaward side of Peveril Downs. The Exton family commissioned Nottingham architect Walter Hickson to build its central section in 1902 and it was extended westwards in 1905, with George Hardy making further additions in 1927. The greatest moment in its history came in secret on the evening of 17 April 1944 when King George VI hosted dinner for Allied generals. Their wake-up calls in the morning came at 04.00 hours, for attendance at Exercise Smash on the other side of the Purbeck Hills, in which Studland beach was the target for assault landings in a major live-fire rehearsal for the D-Day landings. Closure and demolition of the Grosvenor began in 1965 as part of an ambitious plan by Durrant Developments to create a yacht marina and seaside village. The project foundered on the rocks, physically and financially, though some luxury continental-style villas were built in 1987.

Uncertainty also threatened the 1895-built replacement Pier which stretches further into Swanage Bay than its predecessor. The view now belongs to those in window seats in the Mowlem Restaurant (right) with the Brook having been put into a concrete culvert between it and The Parade. The Stone Pier and Marine Villas survive with the stone-walled space behind being the site of the Hotel Grosvenor.

The Mowlem (top left) and Stone Quay (centre left) from Docwra's columns on Peveril Downs.

SWANAGE

Stone Bankers and Mowlem Institute – 1884

Stacks of kerbing and paving of stone merchants Burt and Burt ready for shipment from Swanage. These were locally known as 'the bankers'. Stone Bankers was the formal term to avoid confusion with the other sort of banker. The view is north-eastwards from the new Institute Road to Ballard Point, or Ballard Head as it was locally known (right).

Institute Road takes its name from the Mowlem Institute (far left) which was provided by John Mowlem, at the cost of £1,100 in 1863. The Swanage-born founder of contractors Mowlem and Company made his fortune using kerbing such as this to pave the streets of London. He retired to Swanage where he died in 1868. The Mowlem Institute was 'established for the improvement of the inhabitants in the arts connected with their callings and in the principles of science and useful knowledge generally'. The lecture hall was attached to a reading room with national and local newspapers and a library of 1,450 volumes. The town's Freemasons – of which Mowlem was the first master – held their monthly lodge meetings at the Institute.

Different bankers in Institute Road, in 1922, with Capital and Counties having merged with Westminster and Parr's Bank on the corner (left).

SWANAGE

Institute Road – 2002 (Rodney Legg)

This is as close as you can sensibly get to the 1884 viewpoint, without being run over, or taking a close-up shot of the '3 for £10' tops displayed beside the sign for Cut N Dry'd outside Surprise 'N' Store. This is the angled frontage of Albion Place, with the balcony, which was built in 1896. Immediately behind, four-storey Surfari was built in 1885, as Tatchell's Grocery and Provision Stores on the site of an old shop owned by Martin Cole Ellis. The main line of Edwardian shops in Institute Road, with apartments of The Parade seawards, arose from the hard-core and debris of the Stone Bankers.

The Mowlem Institute was demolished in 1966 and replaced by the three-storey Mowlem Theatre and Restaurant. Rails of a tramway, for hauling stone from the bankers to the old pier, survive in the pavement on the sea wall between The Parade and the Stone Quay. Shops that have come and gone notably included 'house agent' (more honest than estate agent) John Woodford White at No. 1 Institute Road which became a branch of the Capital and Counties Bank in 1915. Having merged with Westminster and Parr's Bank, in 1921, it was as the Westminster Bank, on 17 August 1942, that it was hit by a German bomb. Eight people were killed and 39 injured.

Ice cream and tramway points (bottom right) between The Parade (top right) and the Stone Quay.

SWANAGE

Swanage Station – 1976 (Colin Graham)

The nadir of the Swanage Railway was in 1976, four years after the removal of the permanent way, with an increasing view in the town that Andrew Goltz's revival crusade had both 'stopped in its tracks and run out of steam'. The view from the centre of the main platform at the seaside terminus is north-eastwards to Gilbert Road. Road was winning over rail and coaches were being parked across the former sidings. It seemed likely that Swanage Station had gone the way of Swanage Brewery, on the south side of the railway station, which had produced the renowned Swanage Pale Ale. Panton's Brewery was on the site of Gillingham's Malthouse which was destroyed by fire on 8 November 1854. Rebuilt by James Panton it saw the arrival of the railway in 1885 but then closed and was demolished in 1893.

Swanage Brewery, rebuilt by James Panton after a fire in 1854, pictured in the 1880s.

As for the railway, it nearly went the same way, having only a brief escape from Dr Richard Beeching's axe. A long fight against closure failed in 1972 and the track was lifted with 'indecent haste'. Though the line and buildings were bought by Dorset County Council, hopes of reviving the railway were treated with scepticism, to say the least, by many in Swanage.

SWANAGE

Swanage Station – 2002 (Rodney Legg)

The rejuvenation of Swanage Station was accompanied by the building of Swanage Health Centre in the yard on the site of Panton's Brewery. Something similar might have happened to Swanage Station if negotiations with railway enthusiasts had not resulted in a lease that enabled the Southern Steam Trust and other bodies to bring rescued locomotives to the town – by road – for restoration. Road schemes, however, still threatened the revival of the line even as its track was being re-laid. People in Corfe Castle wanted their section of the line to be used for a by-pass. Not until May 1992 did the National Trust drop its objections to reconstruction of the railway through Corfe to a new station at Norden. Linking with a 3-mile spur of Railtrack metals, at Furzebrook, was finally achieved on 3 January 2002.

Swanage Health Centre is on the site of Panton's Brewery.

It was thirty years to the day after the original withdrawal of passenger services. The Swanage Railway is now 9½ miles in length from Station Road at Swanage to Worgret Junction near Wareham. 'The linking of the Swanage Railway's tracks to the national network is a very significant milestone,' said current chairman Bill Trite. 'That goal has been in our volunteers' sights since the branch line closed. The laying of 6½ miles of track to link up with the Railtrack network and the mainline to London is the culmination of thirty years of struggle.'

SWANAGE
White Swan and Institute Road – 1910

The White Swan (left) and the Round House (centre), looking westwards at the junction of the High Street and Institute Road (right). 'Motorists Drive Slowly' is the sign on the corner of the Round House. Other signs are for 'Institute Road' and 'To the Railway Station'. The boarded-up shop, in which James Haysom had sold fancy goods and toys since 1875, was owned by his widow and daughter. The big sign to the right advertises holiday cars for hire by Thomas Bennett (top) and building contractor Frank Smith. The corner building in the foreground, beside Taunton Road, is the Old Bank House at No. 2 The Square. This was the local branch office of the

The Ship, newly refurbished, on the east side of the Taunton Road junction.

Dorsetshire Bank, managed by William Grove White, who was followed by architects James Clifton and Edmund Robinson. The shop-front was added in 1907 for the old Knitson Dairy which was owned by Charles Curtis. Behind, the sign was above the shop of tobacconist and watch-maker Walter John Bick, who moved into No. 3 The Square in July 1901. Till the retirement of postmaster George Horlock that spring it had been the town's Post Office since 1886.

Dating from around 1700, the White Swan is the oldest surviving building in this part of the town. Ernest Penney was the landlord, from 1893 to 1920. The photographer is standing outside The Ship, dating from about 1820, where the licensee was Charles H. Matthews.

SWANAGE
White Swan and Institute Road – 2002 (Rodney Legg)

Change-over time at two of the three shops that replaced the Round House in 1929. Sweets seems to be a safer line beside the sea as the confectioner's has remained in business.

The Old Bank House and its shop (foreground left) were destroyed by a Luftwaffe bomb, on 23 August 1942, which also badly damaged the Ship Hotel. Five people were killed. The other casualty was a monumental terracotta cow above the blinds on the frontage of Swanage Dairies which was managed by Harry Smith at No. 2 The Square, facing Albion Place. Here the present sign is for 'Pine and Gifts'. Bick's Tobacconist, behind at No. 3 was also damaged by the bomb.

Seawards from The Square to Purbeck Heritage Centre.

TURNERS PUDDLE

Tonerspuddle Farm – 1960 (Rodney Legg)

Another discovery in the family tin of photographs was this print of mine, looking north-eastwards from the ford across the northern arm of the River Piddle, to what since the Middle Ages has been known as Tonerspiddle or Tonerspuddle Farm. It preserves the name of its first 'Turner' – a Norman knight – one Henry Toners. The tiny hamlet still exists as a civil parish, called Turners Puddle, and had Thomas Edward Shaw (also known as Lawrence of Arabia) as its most famous parishioner. His former gamekeeper's cottage, across the heath at Clouds Hill, lies in the other direction. Sitting on the grass in the picture are my parents, Ted and Gladys Legg, and our old Standard Eight was parked to their left outside the church.

The tower of redundant Holy Trinity Church was rebuilt in 1760.

Rev. Leonard W. Cook was rector when Colonel Lawrence died in May 1935, after falling off his Brough Superior motor-cycle in an inexplicable accident involving two boy cyclists and, possibly, a mysterious black car. Cook lived at Affpuddle, to which Turners Puddle had been annexed in 1849, and it was the farmer at Turners Puddle, George King Foster, who gave a firm 'No' when the church was offered the opportunity of housing Eric Kennington's effigy of the national hero that can now to be seen in St Martin's Church at Wareham. Foster was determined that the farm-stead and church should remain a rural backwater. Moreton's rector, Rev. Michael Kinloch, was also appalled at the thought of his church becoming 'a shrine to someone like that' and told his churchwardens: 'Over my dead body!' The irony is that it would have been destroyed as a stray German bomb landed on the church in October 1940. The Bishop of Salisbury came up with Wareham as the compromise proposal.

TURNERS PUDDLE

Tonerspuddle Farm – 2000 (Rodney Legg)

Physically, Turners Puddle remains unchanged at the end of its cul-de-sac road, from Rye Hill at Bere Regis. Legally this moped rider is quite within his rights as the track through the fords not only remains a highway maintainable at public expense but carried C-class status, depicted in yellow, on the last printing of the county roads map. Southwards, however, the main flow of the River Piddle cannot be forded by anything less than a tractor.

Open gate to a closed church, at Turners Puddle in a wall dating from 1859.

These unmade tracks are still in the condition to which they were restored by parish efforts in 1864 and 1865. Firstly the road from Briantspuddle and Throop, across the meadows to Turners Puddle Parsonage, was 'raised and widened'. Then the 'deep watery lane' between Tonerspuddle Farm and the Dairy House was turned into a low causeway. Of its 1,999 acres, 1,132 acres of Turners Puddle were heathland, though much had been planted with Frampton Estate pines, and tanks now train across the Bovington side of the parish. Holy Trinity parish church was one of the first in Dorset to be declared redundant. Sir Gilbert and Lady Violet Debenham made their home in sixteenth-century Tonerspuddle Farm House.

"Gadcliffe, Worborough Bay. C.S.C.

TYNEHAM

Gad Cliff and Brandy Bay, in a pen-and-wash sketch – 1853 (C. M. Colvile)

The view south-eastwards from Worbarrow Tout begins with Gad Cliff and overlooks Brandy Bay, with the next projections of the coast being Hobarrow and Broad Bench, followed by Hen Cliff and the Clavell Tower. Swyre Head is the inland headland, with Hounstout Cliff seawards, and St Alban's Head juts into the English Channel (right).

Gad Cliff takes its name from a quarryman's wedge. Brandy Bay also has an appropriate name, from its active service role in the smuggling era, which ended with six offenders being caught here on the evening of 31 January 1834. Aged from sixteen to thirty-five, they comprised a landing party, caught by Lieutenant Henry John Carr, the Chief Officer of the Coastguard stationed at Kimmeridge. Robert Tent, Joseph Luker, William Short, Robert Manuel, Joseph White and John Strickland were sentenced to death in March 1834, at the Lent Assize in Dorchester. This would be commuted, however, at the Midsummer sessions, to a year's hard labour in each case.

Gated view, south-eastwards from Gad Cliff to St Alban's Head in 1972, before the re-opening of the coast path.

TYNEHAM

Gad Cliff – 2000 (Rodney Legg)

Trying to photograph with an artist's eye is particularly demanding, if not impossible, as it shows how the human eye can enlarge and interpret the detail, whereas the camera pushes it into the background and treats everything proportionately. A telephoto lens brings its own problems, enlarging just one point at a time, and loses the wider picture.

Gad Cliff rises to 450 feet with its line of limestone crags, overlooking the tumbled undercliff of Brandy Bay, providing breeding ledges for seabirds, jackdaws and peregrine falcons. The latter continued to breed on the Lulworth Ranges through the 1970s when poisoning by dioxins, an agricultural chemical, brought it to the brink of extinction. Pesticides and herbicides are not used on the Lulworth Ranges which became one of the greatest reservoirs of wildlife on the South Coast.

Wagon Rock (left), Brandy Bay and the distinctive profile of Gad Cliff, looking westwards from Tyneham Cap.

8470. Tyneham, nr. Corfe Castle.

TYNEHAM

Post Office Row and St Mary's Church – 1937

The centre of Tyneham village, looking north-westwards to the parish church, with a glimpse of Whiteway Hill beyond. The telephone kiosk has been identified for me by Michael Thomas as a K1 Mark 236 box of 1927, of which about 4,500 were erected, with a later roof sign, circa 1929. It stimulated my first ever Tyneham anecdote, from Bournemouth insurance man Wilson Coombes visiting our home in Moordown in 1960, who told me he had installed it in the winter of 1929 and received a tirade of abuse from the rector who resented the modern intrusion.

The Post Office, derelict and engulfed in scrub, in 1972.

On the outbreak of war – Sunday 3 September 1939 – Mrs Gwendoline Driscoll was the shopkeeper at the Post Office (telephone Kimmeridge 221) and stayed in business as the military grip intensified. Beach defences and defenders, behind thousands of mines, faced the threat of German invasion as hard-pressed Warmwell Spitfires fought the aerial war above. A news blackout prevented Tyneham from being given the credit, after a forced-landing on Povington Heath on 11 July 1940, of receiving the first two Germans to be taken prisoner in the Battle of Britain. Then the Royal Air Force requisitioned much of the village as support facilities for a coastal radar station that had been established on the ridge above South Egliston, where author Mary Butts, who died in 1937, had found her rural idyll. It was finally shattered by the secret decision of Churchill's War Cabinet to extend the Lulworth Ranges across the hills and heaths of Tyneham parish in order to train tank crews for the forthcoming Battle of Normandy. Eviction notices were issued by Major General Harvey Miller of Southern Command, on 16 November 1943, requiring them to 'give this further help towards winning the war with a good heart'. Evacuation day was set for the Sunday before Christmas. 'We shall thank you for treating the village kindly,' read the notice villagers left pinned to the church door on 19 December 1943. The last three children to live in the village were Cyril Griffiths, Colin Driscoll and Diana Whitlock.

TYNEHAM

Post Office Row and St Mary's Church – 2000 (Rodney Legg)

Promises that the villagers could return, accepted as such by the Attlee Government in 1947, were never honoured. The campaign on behalf of those who wanted to go home stalled as we realised that former tenants had no legal rights. Freeholders and their heirs had a continuing interest, under the Crichel Down rules, but those we represented were mainly from the wrong side of the social scale. Anno domini was also taking its toll. It led in 1975 to acceptance of a typical British compromise. Tyneham could stay in its remarkable time-warp, with the Army in control, but public access would be provided on a scale unprecedented for active gunnery ranges. So it came to pass. St Mary's Church and the School became museums, ruins were made safe, and coastal footpaths re-opened.

Restored K1 Mark 236 telephone box, with roof sign, of 1929.

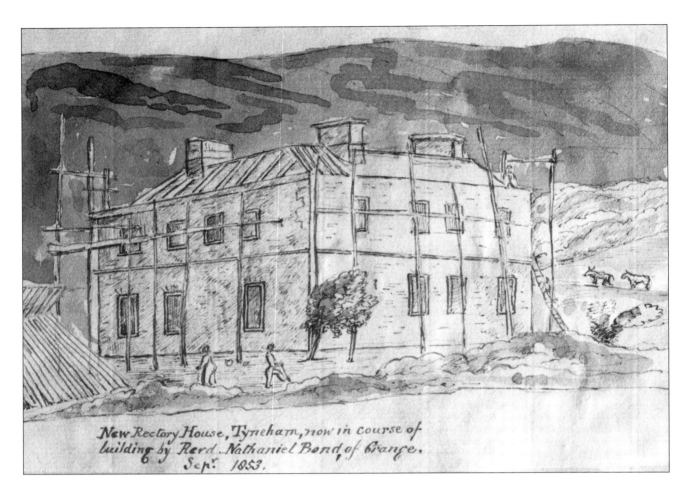

New Rectory House, Tyneham, now in course of building by Revd. Nathaniel Bond, of Grange. Sep'. 1853.

TYNEHAM

The Rectory, in a pen-and-wash drawing — 1853 (C. M. Colvile)

Tyneham Rectory is shown scaffold-clad, during construction, looking north-west towards the Purbeck Hills. The contemporary caption explains: 'New Rectory House, Tyneham, now in course of building by Revd Nathaniel Bond of Grange, September 1853.' Grange was Creech Grange, on the other side of the hill, and the living at Tyneham which went with that of Steeple and East Holme was in Nathaniel Bond's gift. The chosen man in 1889 was Rev. Christopher Wordsworth, son of the Bishop of Salisbury, a scholar who followed in his father's footsteps and became Prebendary of Salisbury Cathedral. During the Great War the rector at Tyneham was Rev. Edward Clifford Hawkes. Rev. Frederick de la Poer Beresford was followed by Rev. Christopher Campbell Sharpe in 1927. Rev. Edwin George Clifford Frend of Wadham College, Oxford, followed from 1933 until his death in 1937.

The Rectory in autumn 1943, also looking north-westwards, with sash windows open.

The last rector was Rev. Humphrey Churchill Money. By 1943 the Rectory had already been requisitioned by the military, initially for accommodation for radar operatives of RAF Brandy Bay, and the rector was serving with the Royal Engineers at Corsham in Wiltshire. As with every building in Tyneham parish it was emptied for the extension of the Lulworth Ranges on 19 December 1943.

TYNEHAM

The Rectory — 2000 (Rodney Legg)

Youths caused a fire in 1966 which gutted the building. When I gave this as an example of how Tyneham had fared in Ministry of Defence care, at a public meeting in Wareham, I was interrupted by a heckler: 'Vandals did that, not the Army!'

'It wouldn't have happened if the rector had still been in residence,' I replied to applause. The building was then reduced to half its height, in 1976, on the excuse of making it safe. It is now accessible, most weekends and during the block leave periods of Christmas and August, when the Lulworth Range Walks are open.

Entrance and south-east corner of the Rectory, as a gutted shell, in 1972.

TYNEHAM

Tyneham House – 1943

Palms flourished around the pond at the back of Tyneham House which is seen in a view looking north-westwards. In terms of age the story runs from left to right. The lower roof-line (left) is that of a mediaeval hall built by the Russel family in the fourteenth century. Henry Williams added a great open fireplace in the eastern room in 1567. The main east-facing range (right) was added in 1583. After the Civil War, Tyneham passed into the ownership of Sir Robert Lawrence of Creech Grange, when he married its heiress, Jane Williams. Their son, John Lawrence, sold it to Nathaniel Bond in 1683, and also parted with the Grange. The Bonds used the two homes in tandem with senior members customarily living at Creech and sons going over the hill to Tyneham. Rev. William Bond rebuilt the Elizabethan main rooms of Tyneham House in 1820 with loftier ceilings and windows.

Ornamental pond, centre of attention for Major Mick Burgess (right), with Head Warden Brian Morgan and John Pitfield (left).

The last owner was William Ralph Garneys Bond. Ralph Bond, born in 1880, served in the Sudan political service and was Governor of Fung and Dongola Provinces. He was accompanied by his loyal servant Said until retirement in 1926. Initially he moved into Woodsford Castle and with hindsight would have stayed there. The return to Tyneham deteriorated by stages. In 1940 he headed Tyneham platoon of the Home Guard. The following year, Tyneham House was requisitioned by the RAF for as officer accommodation for a coastal radar station. Ralph Bond's family moved into the former Coachman's Cottage between Tyneham House and Tyneham Farm. After the total military occupation of 1943 he moved to Moigne Combe, near Crossways, and was High Sheriff of Dorset when the war ended in 1945. Ruination of his Tyneham 'hurt him terribly' and he died in exile at Moigne Combe, in 1952, before he could cash the compensation cheque for his beloved valley.

TYNEHAM

Tyneham House – 1993 (Rodney Legg)

Wall panelling from Tyneham House was taken to Dorset County Museum, in Dorchester, between 1949 and 1951. The house then became increasingly derelict. In 1965 it was reported to the Ancient Monuments Board 'that the Elizabethan part of the house had collapsed internally, following the loss of its roof'. Miss Joyce Melhuish, at the Ministry of Public Buildings and Works, admitted in 1968 that 'the Board eventually decided that salvage of the building as a whole would be an impossibility, and the best that could be done was to allow certain features which were capable of being dismantled and erected elsewhere to be removed from the site'. Ironically, although 'the rest of the fabric has had to be abandoned', the mediaeval hall at the rear was provided with a corrugated iron roof and has survived intact.

The preserved south-west corner of Tyneham House, its mediaeval hall (left), under corrugated iron in 1995.

WAREHAM

North Street – 1882

Southwards along North Street to the Town Hall (centre) which was rebuilt, with a Gothic clock-turret and spire, in 1870. The Greyhound Inn (left) has a side door with the sign 'J. Bridle, Photography'. John Bridle's letterhead claimed a string of civil appointments to go with his main occupations as photographer and publican: 'Town Sergeant, Town Crier, School Attendance Officer, Inspector of Nuisances, and Collector to Urban Sanitary Authority.' Along the left-hand side, at number 16 North Street, author Mrs Dinah Maria Craik wrote part of her novels *Agatha's Husband* and *John Halifax, Gentleman* while staying with clay-pit owner William Joseph Pike in the early 1850s, when she was Miss Mulock.

Glebe House (left) and the former Greyhound Inn.

In the other direction, north of the Greyhound Inn, Glebe House had been built in 1881 and was the home and surgery of medical officer Woodruffe Daniel. Buildings opposite (right) included the remains of All Hallows Chapel. North Street was then dubbed 'Law Street' because of its proliferation of administrative offices, including a courtroom, and a choice of solicitors. They included Philip Edward Lionel Budge (Budge and Slade), Freeland Filliter and George Clavell Filliter (Filliter and Son), Arthur William Pearce, and James Robert Slade (Budge and Slade). The Filliter family lived in St Martin's House which was built to designs by Weymouth architect George Crickmay in 1865. Close to the Town Hall, the Post Office was at number 4 North Street, where John Budden Best had been postmaster since 1868. The Inland Revenue Office, managed by Maurice Collins, was in rooms at the Red Lion. Also in North Street was the registrar of marriages, Albert Laws, and accountant John Murley. There were also carriers including Bartlett and Speed – conveying a sense of urgency – and the modern-sounding Sutton's Parcel Express where the manager was James Oliver Ford. The Red Lion sent a horse-drawn omnibus along North Street to meet the London trains at Wareham Station.

WAREHAM

North Street – 2002 (Rodney Legg)

John Bridle was still at the Greyhound Inn in 1890 but it seems to have been de-licensed during the coming decade. The building survives, however, as number 22 North Street though without the signs it looks much smaller. Shops and flats replaced All Hallows Chapel after its demolition in 1896, and include the inevitable solicitor's office, with Neville-Jones at number 19 (right). The family have been to twentieth-century Wareham what the Filliters were to the eighteenth and nineteenth, in terms of court and coroner services. John Budden Best eventually retired from the Post Office in 1907.

The Town Hall, rebuilt in Victorian Gothic, in 1870.

WAREHAM
The Quay

The New Inn (left) was new in 1785, bearing out my adage that almost all of them can be called old, though a visit to any supermarket will show the power of the word when it comes to branding. Thomas John Hewlett was succeeded as landlord by Alfred Adams. There was also a Rising Sun on the Quay, from 1870 till the 1930s with its landlords around the turn of the century being John White and Charles Chard. Rev. Canon Selwyn Blackett was the rector at Lady St Mary parish church. Though looking empty, the area still had commercial enterprises, including coal merchants Philip Parmiter Gillingham on the Quay and Henry Thorne on Church Green, with the Oakley Brothers as corn merchants at the Granary (right).

This was a busy place in Saxon times. Viking incursions up the Frome are recorded in the *Anglo-Saxon Chronicle*. By tradition, a boat-shaped Purbeck marble coffin in Lady St Mary's Church was used for the burial in 978 of the assassinated King Edward from Corfe Castle. The coffin was found on the site of what is now the King's Chapel. This was built in 802 for the burial of King Brihtic of the West Saxons. He was later exhumed and re-buried at Tewkesbury and Edward was removed to Shaftesbury Abbey and sainthood. Much more would be here in its Wareham setting were it not for the 1841 'restoration' of Lady St Mary's which demolished the best seventh-century building in Europe, though it spared enough for the church to boast what is regarded as the finest surviving Saxon masonry in the country.

The Old Granary (with Mini estate car) and Lady St Mary's tower reflected in the river in 1963.

WAREHAM
The Quay

Leisure is now writ large. Miss P. M. Carter and her friend Miss S. L. J. L. Sydenham established the Old Granary Tea Rooms and Gardens (telephone Wareham 10). The New Inn eventually came of age and ended the millennium as the Quay Inn. The stucco-fronted former warehouse (centre), eighteenth-century No 4 Church Green, looks out on what is now the busiest car-park in town.

The New Inn has come of age as the Quay Inn.

WAREHAM
Saint Martin's Church – 1884 (Walter Pouncy)

The parish of the meadows and heathland beyond the River Piddle continued to carry the name Wareham St Martin though its Saxon church, standing on King Alfred's Town Walls, has been out of use since the eighteenth century. The basic building retains its original walls, as Dorset's earliest complete church, though Saxon arcading was replaced by Norman arches in the twelfth century. A north aisle was also provided and contemporary wall paintings survive. Nothing more of significance was done until 1712 when a towering porch was added to the south front and the royal arms of Queen Anne, dated 1713, were painted over the chancel arch. By 1736, however, it was disused, 'except for marriages, christenings, and the churching of women'. It was then turned into emergency accommodation, with a fireplace, for people dispossessed by the town's big fire of 1762. A century later, in 1861, it was 'now entirely deserted, and unless speedy efforts are made for its preservation, it will be impossible to prevent its complete ruin'.

The ivy had spread by the time of Queen Victoria's golden jubilee celebrations, in 1887.

Nothing was done, saving the building from what would have been destroyed through Victorian restoration, and visiting members of the Dorset Natural History and Antiquarian Field Club in 1907 found 'a general air of forsaken neglect'. They described it as 'a very extraordinary yet interesting effect'. Down the hill, Frederick Green was the landlord of the Lord Nelson, on the east side of the slope above North Bridge. The dray belongs to Panton's Brewery and is heading back to Swanage.

WAREHAM
Saint Martin's Church – 2002 (Rodney Legg)

The two main changes have been the arrival of Lawrence of Arabia's effigy, after his death at Bovington Camp following a motor-cycle accident in 1935, and de-licensing of the Lord Nelson towards the end of the century. The offer of Eric Kennington's flowing sculpture of Colonel Thomas Edward Lawrence as a prince of Mecca had been rejected by each of the parish churches around his Clouds Hill home. None wanted to become a shrine to the most enigmatic of national heroes. Conveniently, St Martin's was at last being repaired – and there were no worshippers to frighten – though the church was rededicated for religious use by the Bishop of Salisbury on 23 November 1936.

Lawrence and dagger, sculpted by Eric Kennington.

WAREHAM

South Bridge – 1912 (C. J. Cornish Brown)

Ancient five-arched South Bridge, Wareham's gateway to the Isle of Purbeck, dated from the eleventh century. Its cut-waters and arches were last rebuilt in 1788 at a cost of £2,932. The view is north-westwards, to the roof of Stephen White Bennett's brewery (centre) and the tower and nave roof of Holy Trinity Church, where county historian John Hutchins was the last rector, in the eighteenth century. The church ceased to be used for services after the big Wareham fire of 1762. Stephen Bennett was also the last of his line, as town brewer and maltster, and retired across the road to Bridge House (centre, right).

With Water Therapy is the boat's name and promise.

Horse-drawn coaches had higher levels of visibility but the hump on the bridge obscured the view for motorised drivers. For a time there was an unofficial signal-man who took it upon himself to stand on the centre arch with red and green flags. There was inevitable pressure for a long-term solution.

WAREHAM

South Bridge – 1996 (Rodney Legg)

The loss of historic South Bridge took place in 1926 to placate the motorists who have since been largely taken out of town by the relief road that crosses the River Frome a mile upstream. Even in the tasteless Twenties there were plenty of protests. Donald Maxwell, writing *Unknown Dorset*, denounced the removal 'of a priceless relic of old Dorset' with the comment that the people of Wareham had the councillors they deserved – 'a lot of dunderheaded, unimaginative, stupid, short-sighted jacks-in-office who, if they had a little more brains, would be half-witted.' Norman footings confirmed the antiquity of the old bridge and the stone was taken away in 1927 for Leonard Sturdy's new house at Trigon. The date-stone over a garage door has the following inscription: 'This Bridge rebuilt 1788.' The concrete replacement, of one main span with two side arches, looked appropriately tacky for years. I noted in 1972, 'dressed white with paint that flakes into the water below'.

As a consequence of the widening of the bridge – more than doubling its width – South Street had to be widened as well. The corner building at the Quay was rebuilt, effectively losing half the space in its former gable-end, and merged with that to its east to form what is now Bridge House Restaurant. The stone wall (far right) disguises public conveniences.

Town pump, moved in 2002, from East Street to its new location opposite Bridge House.

WEST LULWORTH
Durdle Door – 1900

Appreciation of Dorset's remarkable rock-arch came late in the celebration of landscape in the romantic imagination. Visitors from Weymouth, led by King George III, discovered the landscape and charms of Lulworth but the challenging cliff path and inaccessibility to carriages kept Durdle Door a well-kept secret into the nineteenth century. Even Thomas Hardy, using this coast for his smuggling tale *The Distracted Preacher*, failed to mention the now famous rock-arch. Those hired to carry kegs avoided East Chaldon, climbing to 'a lonely trackless place not far from the ancient earthwork called Round Pound. An hour's brisk walking brought them within sound of the sea, not many hundred yards from Lulstead [Lulworth] Cove.' This was at Scratchy Bottom, facing Durdle Door, where a rope was uncoiled from around a smuggler's stomach and dangled from an iron bar driven into the clifftop: 'They all began to descend, partly stepping, partly sliding down the incline, as the rope slipped through their hands.'

South-westwards, to the Isle of Portland, photographed by Rodney Legg in 1967.

The silence of the night was broken by 'the dip of heavy oars, and the dashing of waves against a boat's bow'. The keel crunched into the shingle and the carriers plunged into the water 'as of a brood of ducks' to grab the tubs. The view in our picture is south-eastwards. Avoidance of the rock-arch, with south-westerly winds and waves tending to push craft into its inner corner, would have been in the skipper's mind. It is a key indicator of position along this stretch of cliffs. Added perils are other offshore rocks including the Cow, the Blind Cow and the Bull to the west. Eastwards, towards Dungy Head, the Man o'War and Norman Rock and a folk memory of shipwrecks make St Oswald's Bay even more dangerous.

WEST LULWORTH
Durdle Door – Colin Graham (1982)

Where Hardy failed his film-makers succeeded brilliantly. An enduring image from John Schlesinger's classic *Far from the Madding Crowd*, from 1967, has Terence Stamp as Sergeant Francis Troy, faking his disappearance into the sea beside Durdle Door. Hardy had used Lulworth Cove as his setting.

Cliffside obelisk, one of two nautical beacons, showing the approach into Portland Harbour.

The wash of the sea on fine shingle make this a geographical and nautical feature as timeless as ever, though now it is one of the best known features in British landform geology. It played its part in achieving World Heritage Site status for most of the Dorset coast in 2001. The name Durdle derives from an Old English word 'thirled' for 'holed' with such sounds having been given a 'd' in the Dorset dialect. The same origin explains the Thurlestone in Devon. Clifftop beacons west of Bat's Head, two concrete pointers, line up to bear 048 degrees to indicate the approach across Weymouth Bay for the East Ship Channel into Portland Harbour. Not a lot of people know that.

Lulworth Cove, near Weymouth.

WEST LULWORTH
Lulworth Cove – 1905

Another Lulworth scene that hardly changed during the twentieth century is world-famous Lulworth Cove, with even the paddle-steamer making nostalgic returns, when the Clyde-based *Waverley* comes down south on her summer excursions. The view, with a visiting Weymouth steamer, is eastwards to Bindon Hill. The rounded basin is sheltered, except in southerly winds, which push a heavy swell through the entrance (right). It is relatively shallow, with a depth of 12 feet in the middle, and though this would normally only be suitable for small craft the paddle-steamers were exceptional in drawing very little water. The entrance is a cable in width.

Beach weather, southwards to the cove entrance.

The busiest time in its history was early in the Iron Age, from about 500 BC, when Celtic immigrants from France fortified the length of Bindon Hill with a stout rampart. Their east-facing alternative landing beach was in Mupe Bay. Nothing much happened for another couple of millennia. Oyster, crab and lobster fishermen were puzzled at the adoption of the 'southern spas' by the social set immortalised by playwright John O'Keeffe who found the original for his John Barleycorn in *William Randall* at the old Red Lion Inn in West Lulworth. George III visited on excursions from sea-bathing at Weymouth. The poet John Keats, on his final journey to Rome on 30 September 1820, spent his last hours on English soil at Lulworth after the *Maria Crowther* put into the cove while awaiting a favourable wind. Thomas Hardy commemorated the visit with a centennial poem. Lulworth Cove also features in Thomas Hardy's novels as Lulstead (or Lulwind) Cove. Soldier-poet Rupert Brooke also wrote about Lulworth coincidences and called it 'the most beautiful place in England'. Fate dealt a most un-Hardy like series of miracles to an eleven-year-old girl who fell 380 feet down the chalk cliff from the top of Bindon Hill (left) on 7 September 1892. Having survived despite 'terrible injuries' she was carried to the Coastguard boathouse. There her life was saved by royal surgeon Sir Frederick Treves. He was in Lulworth 'reading a book written by her father' when 'the alarm reached my cottage'.

WEST LULWORTH
Lulworth Cove – 2000 (Rodney Legg)

Stormy waters, breaking white on either side of the entrance, westwards from Pepler's Point.

My attempt at replicating the picture is a 'joiner'. I had the wrong lens for managing with a single shot. The exposed chalk on Bindon Hill (top left) has become steadily greener throughout the half century I have known it. Red danger flags along the far shore mark the boundary of the Lulworth Ranges though it is accessible when the paths are open at weekends and holidays.

HIGH STREET, WINFRITH.

WINFRITH NEWBURGH
High Street – 1930

The view is northwards along the High Street from Weston Cottage (left) and the Forge (far right) to Crown Corner beside the junction with School Lane (centre). These are the nineteenth-century buildings at the centre of Winfrith village, linking an older grouping of homes to the north with the ancient part of the village to the south. Crown Corner and Crown Yard preserve the memory of the former Crown Inn. At the other end of the picture, blacksmith Henry Cox was well positioned both for the village trade and that which came down the hill, along

The Post Office in 1930, at the north end of the High Street, looking north-eastwards from Thornicks.

Winfrith Drove, from the downlands towards Lulworth. Buildings tend to gather in character and age towards Winfrith Fields Farm, dating from Tudor times, where the farmhouse is also known as the Manor House. This was the home of the Newburgh family who left the parish their name. The street ends at this point, forking into lanes either side of St Christopher's parish church, which has visible antiquity with twelfth-century masonry beside its outer doorway and the inner entrance to the chancel.

Winfrith House lies behind trees to the left, with a battlemented gatehouse facing Winfrith Drove which joins the High Street from the east, beside the Forge. The eighteenth-century mansion was the home of Frederick Allan Scott Colquhoun, followed by Captain Bridgeman Alexander and Mrs M. A. Stopford Adams.

WINFRITH NEWBURGH
High Street – 2002 (Rodney Legg)

A smithy no longer, Forge Cottage houses Peter and Susan Hyde. The Post Office, which used to be in the most northern house on the east side of the High Street, has moved southwards into this view, to the shop just beyond Crown Corner.

Wall ties holding stone and brick at Winfrith Fields.

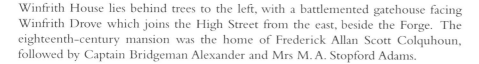

The High Street to the south of the corner beside the Forge (centre).

THORNICKS, WINFRITH.

WINFRITH NEWBURGH
Thornicks and Winbrook – 1930

The stream from East Chaldon runs at the bottom of the long gardens along the western side of the High Street before running beside the road at Thornicks. The view is south-westwards along Winbrook to Riverside (right) and numbers 34 to 37. The former is from the seventeenth century, with low ceilings and a central fireplace, and the adjoining cottage a century later.

The Winbrook flowing into the village beside the Manor House.

WINFRITH NEWBURGH
Thornicks and Winbrook – 2002 (Rodney Legg)

Bridging the ford might seem to have been the biggest change in these parts, apart from industrial buildings having appeared behind the photographer in Winbrook Fold, but something significant happened over the horizon to the right, a mile away, though you can visit Winfrith Newburgh without realising it. Clusters of cottages such as this can still be found across the parish, including East Knighton hamlet and the Blacknoll, on the edge of Winfrith Heath nature reserve which has been established by Dorset Wildlife Trust.

Beyond this are the buildings, towers and reactors of the Atomic Energy Establishment which dominate the skyline towards the River Frome. The go-ahead for the 1,100-acre site of 'a second Harwell' was given in 1957 which was the year of a leak from Windscale that resulted in it being re-named Sellafield. 'Operation Windfall' would be the local alarm if the time came for taking potassium iodine tablets to protect the thyroid gland from absorbing radiation. Experimental SGHWR (Steam Generated Heavy Water Reactor) and DRAGON (High Temperature Reactor sponsored by the Organization for Economic Cooperation and Development) sites, both since shut-down, have followed by new roles for the land inside the perimeter fence. Surplus buildings became the new headquarters for Dorset Police in the late 1970s. Electricity generation ceased in 1990 and tritium recycling from luminous telephones stopped in 1995. Nearby East Knighton, the only community beside the main road that crosses the parish, used to be the busiest spot hereabouts, and it used to be pointed out to me that it housed distant Legg and Kerley. The Rising Sun has since become the Countryman.

The nuclear skyline beyond Blacknoll.

Towards the other end of the parish, within sight of Daggers Gate, Marley Wood Cottage was a former rustic combination of barn and cottage under the same roof, converted into a modern house by Bill and Pru Wintrip in 1980.

WOOL

Spring Street – 1902 (Walter Pouncy)

Grassy and wide Spring Street was the main road through Wool village, rather than the present High Street to the west, which used to be a narrow back street. The view is southwards from outside Charles Podger's shop in the business quarter around the Cross. The cart has come to a halt outside George Thomas's smallholding at Sexys Farm. The adjoining thatched cottage to the right is number 49 Wool, to give it the rent-book identification in the Weld Estate records. F. W. Manuel was the last tenant when the 'Wool Portion' of the estate was auctioned by Alfred Savill and Sons at Dorchester on 12 September 1925. Next-door number 50, Stanley Cottage, was bought by its tenant, William Langford. The Langfords were boot-makers, builders and shopkeepers.

Detailed view, Stanley Cottage to Wool Farm, from the stream (foreground).

Wool Farm, operated by Charles Hyde on the corner with Church Lane, was bought back from the family estate by Herbert Joseph Weld of Lulworth Castle. Beyond it is the tower of Holy Rood parish church. Looking out of place amid the rusticity (right) is a neat Georgian house, Seaforth Cottage, which looks like has strayed from the promenade of a seaside spa. It had personalities to match in the form of the Misses Penney. Their male equivalent was Major Bertram Edmund Freame, the land steward, for the Lulworth Estate.

WOOL

Spring Street – 2002 (Rodney Legg)

The corner around the Cross is now the preserve of Williams the Baker, which accounts for the parked van (right). The timber-built Cremona Tea Rooms has come and gone. Otherwise, apart from the cars and farming activities having moved out of the village, Spring Street is as perfect as ever. There is an abundance of cottage garden plants and the angle hides the best bit of the setting which is the stream.

Another thatched corner, downstream and north-eastwards, from the entrance to Sexys Farm.

Further along the street is the Poor House Barn, an eighteenth-century brick and cob building 60 feet in length, which was saved in July 1975 when the village went into a state of revolt and protesters' cars blocked the road to prevent its demolition. They saved the day, because the contractors failed to get their equipment through, and had only managed to remove a few tiles when planning officer Douglas Young arrived from Purbeck District Council. He stuck a newly issued 'Preserved building' notice on the door. ' The barn is said to have been used as a sleeping place for poor travellers,' Wellington-booted Pat McCullagh told me, his ancient coat held together with binder-twine and the remains of pockets dangling loose. He looked the part as a prospective user but after his death, in 1996, we heard he was a millionaire and had left most of his fortune to charity, including a £20,000 bequest to the parish council.

WOOL

Woolbridge Manor and Wool Bridge, in a water-colour – 1904
(Raphael Tuck)

The view is looking northwards, across the River Frome, to Jacobean Woolbridge Manor and mediaeval Wool Bridge. Internationally, this has to be the best known Dorset setting, always in thousands of minds, thanks to Thomas Hardy choosing it for the crucial turn of fate that befalls heroine Tess Durbeyfield as Angel Clare's bride in *Tess of the d'Urbervilles*. The compelling thing about Woolbridge Manor is that it came to Hardy with its traditions intact and he only had to add the characters. Not only was there a spectral coach, said to be visible only to those with Turberville blood in their veins, but Hardy himself saw the plaster-painted portraits of two 'most brutalised women of a fleshy type, with enormous noses and supercilious mouths' in half-light in Woolbridge Manor. Ruins of Bindon Abbey, on the other side of Wool Bridge, conveniently provided an open stone tomb lying in the grass, where Tess 'stretched herself out at full length in the abbot's old coffin'. Nearby, water thunders under a timber footbridge beside the wheel of Bindon Mill, awesome in daylight and frightening at night.

The upstream, westwards to Woolbridge Manor, from the former railway bridge.

Tess, the best-selling novel which turned fifty-one-year-old Thomas Hardy from a struggling novelist into a famous one, also brought trans-Atlantic rewards, having coincided with the passing of a Copyright Act by Congress. Produced in instalments for *Graphic* editor Arthur Locker in 1891 it appeared as a book the following year. It not only made Hardy rich but the tapestry of easily identifiable Dorset locations, including Bere Regis and Marnhull, started a process that led to the county being called 'Hardy Country'. Rebekah Owen, a wealthy American, was the first Hardy tourist to talk her way into Max Gate and be taken by Emma and Thomas Hardy to ask farmer Henry Peach to show them the portraits in Woolbridge Manor.

Transportation threat, dating from 1820, though Hardy failed to use the story line.

WOOL

Woolbridge Manor and Wool Bridge – 1997 (Rodney Legg)

Hardy was the right name for a durable reputation. If anything, after a century of fame reinforced by film and television, he is now more widely acclaimed than during his lifetime. Tragic Tess remains his best known character.

Its key setting also survives, if only in winter, as summer leaves on the willows obliterate the view of what for a short time was Woolbridge Manor Hotel. The graceful five-arch bridge, last restored in 1688, is now in retirement. The replacement is to the east. Between them a railway line and bridge, taking tanks to Bovington, have come and gone.

Wool Railway Station.

WOOL

Wool Station – 1915

Contractors give the points a safety check in the summer of 2002.

The railway station at Wool, westwards from the up-line signal, during the Great War. Postcard views came into sudden demand with the arrival of hundreds of soldiers following the development of Bovington Camp to the north and Lulworth Camp to the south, through the second half of the conflict, for a new weapons-system called the tank. It was the Tank Corps in those days as the royal cachet was not added until 1923. Passengers crossed the line (foreground) from station buildings beside the down-line (left) to the London-bound platform (right).

The line opened on 1 June 1847 and the goods siding (left) stayed in use until 1965. Military traffic included more than just the personnel. German prisoners-of-war built a 2-mile railway from sidings east of Wool Station, across a concrete and steel bridge downstream of Wool Bridge, to Bovington Camp. It did not come into use until 9 August 1919. The war was over but it was needed more than ever, as the tanks were coming home from the Western Front, to a huge Tank Park across the heath between Bovington and Clouds Hill. Most were eventually broken-up. This line stayed in use for collections of scrap until 4 November 1928, and its rails were also lifted for the furnace, in 1936. Wool Station was provided with a footbridge between the wars. It became a commuter stop in the late 1950s, for white and blue-collar workers from Dorchester and the Bournemouth conurbation, following the building of the Atomic Energy Establishment on nearby Winfrith Heath.

WOOL

Wool Station – 2002 (Rodney Legg)

The Poole train pulling out on the up-platform at Wool.

Though it may not look like it, my modern picture is from the same spot, the difference having been caused by the lengthening of both platforms at the end of the steam era. The last day of mainline steam in the British Isles was on this line, from Weymouth to Waterloo, coinciding with George Stephenson's birthday, on 9 July 1968. Rumours abounded that British Railways wanted to end the railway system at Bournemouth, which were not helped by the demolition of Wool Station and its replacement by what looks like a bus-shelter. The line turned the corner, however, in the following decade with electrification being accompanied by a programme of lengthening the platforms to take more coaches. It was good news for everything apart from the badgers whose traditional paths crossed the tracks in dozens of places between Wool and Dorchester. Beware of imitating an anorak if you go train-spotting after a high-profile rail crash. I was ushered back behind the yellow line. Observing contractors checking the points was becoming something like mustering the Taleban for a farewell photo-call.

WORBARROW BAY

Arish Mell Gap – 1934 (Ted Legg)

The view is eastwards from the 400-feet contour on Cockpit Head, across chalk cliffs and the Arish Mell Gap, to downland slopes at Holcombe Vale, below Rings Hill and Flower's Barrow hill-fort. My father's notebook of family outings, from Easter Road in Bournemouth a decade before I was born, gives the date as 18 June 1934. This coastal scenery between Lulworth and Kimmeridge, as spectacular as any in Dorset, was soon to go out-of-bounds. Dragon's Teeth and a minefield came first, in 1940, followed by an extension of the Lulworth Ranges to take in Sea Vale Farm, Monastery Farm and Holcombe Vale. Monastery Farm was built by the Weld family as a refuge for French Trappist monks during the upheavals. War Premier Winston Churchill stood on Holcombe Vale slopes on 6 April 1942 to review lines of his own newly-developed tank – the Churchill. The range boundary was then extended much further eastwards, across the 3,003-acre entirety of Tyneham parish, on 19 December 1943.

Steer relaxing on the beach at Arish Mell, with a vehicle parked behind, in 1934.

My father, when talking nostalgically about Arish Mell, always mentioned cows on the beach, as did George Adkins of Wimborne who also had a photograph to prove the point. His photograph shows seven bullocks lying on the shingle beside the stream that trickles across the beach. Purbeck coastal history invariably involves smuggling and shipwrecks. To mention an example of each, the Riding Officer from Kimmeridge, Thomas Croombs, was 'beaten and bruised in a very cruel manner' when he intercepted smugglers unloading tea and tobacco from a boat beached at Arish Mell. The vessel washed up on the shingle at the turn of the twentieth century was an iron steamship.

WORBARROW BAY

Arish Mell Gap – 1983 (Colin Graham)

The deeper view from Cockpit Head is across Arish Mell Gap and eastwards to Flower's Barrow, Worbarrow Tout and the cliffs to St Alban's Head. By 1975 the Ministry of Defence was putting into effect a public access package to defuse calls for the release of the Lulworth Ranges, after campaigners including myself had made our peace with Major-General Roy Redgrave, Commandant of the Royal Armoured Corps. The restored path, however, diverts a short distance inland from the beach at Arish Mell, which remains forbidden. That results from it having been chosen in 1956 for the emergency drainage outfall from the Atomic Energy Establishment on Winfrith Heath. A submarine pipeline runs two miles out to sea with a yellow and black warning buoy with a red quick-flashing light three cables south of the seaward end. I succeeded in having a question asked about it in Parliament. These days even radio-active cows are absent from Arish Mell.

Steamship beached at Arish Mell, in about 1899, with the chalk cliff of Cockpit Head rising to the west.

WORBARROW BAY

Worbarrow – 1936

Worbarrow hamlet, from the Bungalow and Sheepleaze to Sea Cottage and the boathouses, north-eastwards from Worbarrow Tout to Baltington (top). The site of the Coastguard Station can be seen to the right of the track inland to Tyneham village. The cliffside Bungalow, above multi-coloured exposures of Wealden sands, was built by Mary Jane Wheeler. It was then the home of Miss M. Hills and was occupied by Squadron Leader C. C. Brachi from Boxmoor, Hertfordshire, in 1943. Sheepleaze, the modern stone-built house on the cliffs, was the holiday home of oil executive Philip Draper from Albury in Surrey. Sea Cottage was the home of Jack and Alice

Boathouse (right) and Sea Cottage (left), northwards to the Bungalow (centre) and Sheepleaze (top right).

'Miggie' Miller. Jack's cousin, Joe Miller – another fisherman – was also living at Sea Cottage, with a stuffed cat in the living room window.

More Millers lived a short distance inland. Charlie Miller, brother of Joe, lived with Harriet in Fern Hollow beside the Gwyle stream which flows down the valley through a gully from Tyneham village. Harriet had been the last Tyneham schoolmistress until its closure, due to falling attendance, in 1932. Tom Miller and wife Minnie lived in Hill Cottage, on the slope of Gold Down, above the footings of the Coastguard Station. Unmarried sisters Beatrice and Winifred Mintern had a smallholding at Worbarrow. Albert Longman was the farmer at Baltington.

WORBARROW BAY

Worbarrow (site of) – 2000
(Rodney Legg)

The former hamlet at Worbarrow, comprising the seaward end of the Tyneham Range and an overshoot and safety zone for tank firing practice on the inland Heath Range of the Gunnery School of the Royal Armoured Corps. All of the inhabitants of Worbarrow along with Povington and Tyneham had to leave their homes in 1943 for the extension of the Lulworth Ranges, and were never allowed to return.

Boathouse (left) and Sea Cottage, north-westwards across Worbarrow Bay to Arish Mell, in the autumn of 1943.

WORTH MATRAVERS
Post Office and Village Green – 1897

The centre of the village at Worth Matravers, looking eastwards from beside the Post Office, in the time of grocer and postmaster Ralph Pushman who returned to his Purbeck roots. The village shopkeeper had been John Turner, and the closest Post Office was in the neighbouring village of Langton Matravers, with letters for Worth being sorted in Wareham. Ralph Pushman changed all this. Born in Swanage, into an old quarrying family which appears in parish records from the fourteenth century onwards, Ralph followed the stone trade to London at a time when it was going through its Victorian renaissance as capital of the British Empire. In 1885 he emigrated to Australia and married Georgina Lucy Mears in Melbourne, in 1891, before returning to Worth via a spell on Dorset's other stone island at Portland. Having acquired the village store he turned it into the Post Office. Letters were received via Langton Matravers, through the week, at 7.45 am and 5.35 pm. Outgoing mail was collected at 9.30 am and 6.50 pm on weekdays and 9.30 on Sundays. The Post Office later became the heart of the community in other ways when Ralph Pushman's daughter, Miss Olive M. Pushman, took over as village midwife. They both lived in the Post Office, into the 1930s, and shared the same telephone number (Corfe Castle 38). Ralph's grandson, Purbeck writer David Pushman, lives in The Hyde at Langton Matravers.

Across the road, behind a stone wall, the village green on the slope has an attractive duck pond and is overlooked by a range of stone-roofed cottages.

Cottages above the village green, reflected in the pond at Worth Matravers.

WORTH MATRAVERS
Post Office and Village Green – 2002 (Rodney Legg)

Not much has changed, except that the Post Office has been taken over by the Ralls family of Christine, David and Derek, and the parking problem has become chronic as visitors and those who should know better ignore the restrictions. Standing around on top of the wall, as one does, I waited for the situation to improve but the world and his wife began arriving in white camper vans with bicycles slung on the back. Part of the attraction was that the building in the immediate foreground (left) has been refurbished as a tea-room.

Around the corner, from the yard in front of the current Charles Newman's Square and Compass Inn, came the sound of chipping stone. Purbeck's masons and sculptors were displaying their craft. The tools of the trade, creaking above on the sign, are symbols of the United Fraternity of Free and Accepted Masons of England. The previous Charlie Newman attracted a wider clientele with quarryman Billy Winspit, on his violin, entertaining Bohemian artist Augustus John and accompanying harem.

Chipping away under the Masonic sign of the Square and Compass.

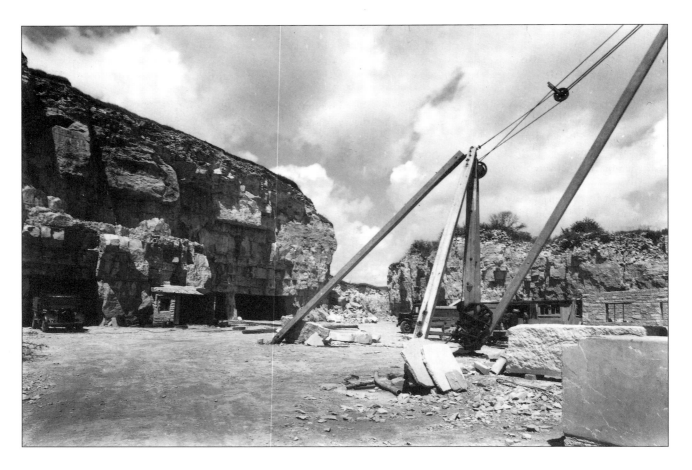

WORTH MATRAVERS
Winspit Quarry – 1938

The working floor of Winspit Quarry with its lorry (background left), buildings and derrick, looking northwards from above the sea. Cliff quarry galleries, here 12 feet in height, extend deep into West Man (left) which is a rounded hill, on limestone downland, terraced with the mediaeval strip-lynchet cultivation strips of extensive open fields which covered both sides of Winspit Bottom.

Here I met its last quarryman, whose story was told in the *Dorset Year Book*: 'Two weeks after I called on him to write this article, Billy Winspit collapsed while working in his garden. He died four days later – on 9 August 1966 – only days short of his eightieth birthday. Though he lived in a remote valley, Billy was perhaps the most well-known character in Purbeck.' His proper name was William Jeremiah Bower but everyone knew him as Billy Winspit. He started in the quarry at the age of eleven and became its blacksmith, sharpening the tools, at a time when pay was 25 shillings a week: 'Out of £11 I used to pay the men's wages.' The base-bed and whit-bed, the latter 7-feet thick, were worked at Winspit. Twelve-ton blocks were still being cut at Winspit with hammers, punches and wedges when this picture was taken, and 15-ton blocks had been removed from along the coast at Seacombe, where the whit-bed was a foot thicker. Seacombe closed between the wars but Winspit had a respite during the Second World War, providing thousands of tons of hard-core for airfields and roads, after which only Billy Winspit stayed on, producing the centre-piece for a stone fireplace in his garden workshop on the day that I visited.

Quarry galleries, 12 feet high, go deep into West Man.

WORTH MATRAVERS
Winspit Quarry – 2002 (Rodney Legg)

The cliff galleries (left) are still standing here, but have collapsed to the west, and derelict buildings (right) date from the Second World War. Rock pools down to the right now resound to holiday sounds but a memorial stone on the cliff is a reminder that this can be a dangerous place to play. Eighteen-year-old Alastair Ian Campbell Johnstone drowned at Winspit on 19 August 1935: 'He loved birds and green places and the wind on the heath and saw the brightness of the skirts of God.'

Winspit westwards, across the rock pools, to West Man.

WYTCH FARM
Oilfield Site X – 1973 (British Gas Council)

Oilfield Site X (for Exploration), south-east of Wytch Farm, looking eastwards into Purbeck Forest on Rempstone Heath, in a far-away part of the 5,123-acre Rempstone Estate owned by Major Dudley Ryder of Rempstone Hall. Much of the land was leased to the Forestry Commission but the Ryder family retained the mineral rights. The Gas Council (Exploration) Limited carried out seismic survey work on the Purbeck heathlands beside Poole Harbour in the winter of 1970.

They hit the bull's eye in this clearing beside Poole Harbour. Six weeks of drilling at Site X was followed by the circulation of this photograph and a cautious press release by the Gas Council (Exploration) Limited. Initial calculations of the oil reserve were for an output of 200,000 tonnes a year (0.2 per cent of national oil consumption) with the oilfield around Wytch Farm having an operating life from 1975 through to between 1990 and 1995. Both were to prove conservative estimates. More oil was found in Purbeck in 1974 than in the whole of Texas.

WYTCH FARM
Oilfield Site X – 1995 (Rodney Legg)

The rest is history. This was how the land was cleared and restored, with installations of the longer-term X Site being visible in the distance (right), beside the access road from the Gathering Station to nodding donkey beam-pumps on Shotover Moor and at Ower.